Tooning In

Tooning In

Essays on Popular Culture and Education

Cameron White
and
Trenia Walker

ROWMAN & LITTLEFIELD PUBLISHERS, INC.
Lanham • Boulder • New York • Toronto • Plymouth, UK

ROWMAN & LITTLEFIELD PUBLISHERS, INC.

Published in the United States of America
by Rowman & Littlefield Publishers, Inc.
A wholly owned subsidiary of The Rowman & Littlefield Publishing Group, Inc.
4501 Forbes Boulevard, Suite 200, Lanham, Maryland 20706
www.rowmanlittlefield.com

Estover Road
Plymouth PL6 7PY
United Kingdom

British Library Cataloguing in Publication Information Available

Library of Congress Cataloging-in-Publication Data

Tooning in : essays on popular culture and education / Cameron White and
Trenia Walker.
  p. cm.
Includes bibliographical references.
ISBN-13: 978-0-7425-5969-1 (cloth : alk. paper)
ISBN-10: 0-7425-5969-6 (cloth : alk. paper)
ISBN-13: 978-0-7425-5970-7 (pbk. : alk. paper)
ISBN-10: 0-7425-5970-X (pbk. : alk. paper)
 1. Education—Social aspects—United States. 2. Popular culture—United States.
3. Education in popular culture—United States. 4. Critical pedagogy—United
States. I. Walker, Trenia, 1965– II. Title.
 LC191.4.W55 2007
 306.43'2—dc22   2007020343

Printed in the United States of America

♾™ The paper used in this publication meets the minimum requirements of
American National Standard for Information Sciences—Permanence of Paper
for Printed Library Materials, ANSI/NISO Z39.48-1992.

Contents

1

Tooning In

Engaging Popular Culture for Social Efficacy in Education

What is the role of schools in promoting social efficacy? How do current practices in education and the teaching and learning process impact social efficacy? What is the role of popular culture in society? Does popular culture have a role in the education process of our young? Is there a connection between popular culture and social efficacy? Popular culture is at the center of societal controversy and debate at present. Many from one end of the spectrum criticize its very nature and suggest that it only serves to destroy American morals and values. These folks call for increased censorship and the like. Many on the other end of the spectrum also criticize the nature of popular culture and suggest that it perpetuates the status quo and enhances corporate and American hegemony. These folks call for more openness and less corporate domination of our culture.

We need to acknowledge that popular culture is part of our lives and is important to our society, our citizens, and especially our children. In a society increasingly fragmented by debate, misunderstandings, and lack of consensus, perhaps popular culture remains one of the few arenas that provide a forum for common understandings, dialog, and communication. If this is so, we need to better integrate popular culture in the education process to enhance popular advocacy if for nothing else. It is precisely in the diverse spaces and spheres of popular culture that most of the education that matters today is taking place on a global scale (Giroux 1994).

The overt goal of our schools is to enhance knowledge, skills, and values development for our children. Unfortunately these goals are too often top-down and authoritarian and promote passivity. These goals therefore seem to be driven by the purpose of preparing our youth for the world of work. This is a realistic goal for schools but should not be the driving force. Ultimately, we must prepare children for active participation as global citizens, which means that we have a responsibility to teach for social efficacy.

Popular culture is a natural phenomenon that is often driven and dictated by the dominant culture. The idea is to critically analyze these issues and also in this way provide the critical efficacy children need to facilitate this natural desire and wonder for learning about and coping with their world. This is vital if we are to employ popular culture and childhood desire to promote social efficacy and social justice attitudes among our children.

EDUCATION FOR SOCIAL EFFICACY

What is meant by teaching and learning for social efficacy? Social efficacy in education moves beyond traditional practice by suggesting the inclusion of student- and issue-centered approaches to teaching and learning. Advocates for social efficacy in education suggest that our schools are often demeaning and disempowering places where children are either bored into submission or where transmission and socialization techniques destroy any hope for critical thinking and problem solving development. The opportunity for teaching for social efficacy that promotes popular culture in schools is great, but we must discard the traditional transmission model of education and schooling in favor of a transformational model (Jennings 1994).

Many see social efficacy and empowerment as a major component of social education curriculum and instruction in our schools. The contention is that traditional social studies education may very well be the bad guy in this debate, for the history of social studies traditionally has been to perpetuate the status quo and often only allows one viewpoint regarding history. With the focus on imposed knowledge and skills and the growing accountability movement, social studies education remains reactionary so as to placate critics. Debate within social studies rarely includes social efficacy or issues-oriented curriculum. The debate has been on what content should be taught and how that content should be covered. A curriculum is needed that encourages participation, critical analysis, and action (Westheimer and Kahne 1998).

The standardization and accountability movements are the culprits. The concepts of critical thinking, problem solving, and issues-centered education are antithetical to this movement. If we encourage children to question and investigate themes and issues in depth, then the status quo and hegemonic powers may well be threatened. These methods now dominate the education process in this country. Ultimately, the goal seems to be to ensure that teaching and learning (at the very least) remain focused on transmission of essential knowledge, skills, and values. We seem to be attempting to standardize our children. Free market capitalism replacing democracy as the governmental ideal is perpetuated by these endeavors. In a democratic society, social studies should provide fodder for dialog and critical analysis of this essential knowledge, skills and values curriculum, and instruction. A social justice approach is critical of transmission, essential knowledge, and the ideal of free market capitalism, and thus is antithetical to the standardization and accountability movements (Chomsky 2000).

Teaching for social efficacy is a strategy for countering the threat enveloping our schools and society. We preach the joys of being a democratic society, yet democracy often cannot be found in our schools. We claim to be an open and just country, but school praxis has virtually turned our schools into prisons. Kids are prisoners subjected to the whims of the school bureaucracy, and teachers have become the guards. Kids are in school to be molded into appropriately acting citizens. These citizens go along with the crowd, pleased as punch to be living in the greatest country in the world.

Teaching for social efficacy suggests that personal stories and controversy be returned to social studies education. It suggests that life and learning is full of controversy and that we owe it to our kids to allow for investigating of social issues, past, present, and future. The premise is that a society not open and comfortable enough to allow for critique cannot progress and is a society in decline. Where is the democracy is this? *Lies My Teacher Told Me* (Loewen 1995) is an excellent chronicle of these issues, particularly regarding history education and history textbooks. Unfortunately (or fortunately, depending on one's point of view), the truly meaningful and lifelong connections in social efficacy have been provided outside of the classroom, especially outside of the social studies classroom. This is the real issue. Can there—and should there—be a school and education connection between social efficacy and popular culture?

Many progressive educators bemoan popular culture in our society as demeaning, hegemonic, corporate dominated, and bad for our kids. Many state emphatically that popular culture runs counter to social efficacy in education. An entire movement called popular literacy has arisen to counter this perception. Any incorporation of popular culture in teaching for social efficacy must obviously bring in critical analysis as a primary tool. The fact remains however, that popular culture is an ideal theme for teaching and learning, both as a possibility for liberation and to discuss its use as a tool for empowerment.

POPULAR CULTURE FOR SOCIAL EFFICACY

What is the connection we all seem to have with popular culture? If we are truly interested in providing meaning to kids' lives as we engage in teaching and learning, why don't we do a better job of integrating popular culture into education? As noted earlier, popular culture is rife with controversy and currently receives strong criticism from all areas of the political spectrum. Much of the criticism is warranted, yet despite political leanings there seems to be general agreement regarding the underlying problems with popular culture and its impact on society and especially our children. What are not needed are simplistic generalizations calling for censorship or attempts at ignoring the influence of popular culture.

Popular culture has never been so dominant in our lives, yet it is experiencing severe criticism. Many are at a loss at how to deal with its influence. A strong argument can be made that popular culture has become the most influential education institution for our children in society, and many seem quite frustrated by this. Rather than fight to ensure one's own agenda in popular culture, it might be better to use it as an educational opportunity.

In many instances, equate popular culture must be equated with childhood desire. Our children's natural desire to make sense of their world can be enhanced through the appreciation and application of popular culture as a pedagogical tool. Popular culture can provide the common connections and voice for what many of us remember as wide-eyed joy and a sense of wonder of the world. Our children must be engaged in this endeavor however; we cannot allow for corporate dictate of this desire through Big Brother or Clockwork Orange–style popular saturation and or brainwashing. Social education that integrates social efficacy is aware and unafraid of childhood desire, often connecting it to children's efforts to understand the world and themselves (Steinberg and Kincheloe 1997).

Our society has made popular culture a cornerstone of cultural identity. Television, movies, and music provide fodder for connections among our disconnected citizenry. Why not use this, rather than belittle it? We owe it to our kids to provide opportunities for critical analysis of popular culture. Rather than blindly accepting the Disneyfication or Simpsonizing of our kids and their lives, use them as teachable opportunities. Using Disney and other animated films, such as *Shrek, Monsters Inc.,* and *Finding Nemo,* to analyze gender and cultural stereotypes may provide for eye-opening experiences for students. Using *The Simpsons* to look at social issues rather than as pure entertainment, for example, can turn kids on to the power and possibilities in popular culture and social justice. Film, television, music, and other forms of popular culture can provide rich opportunities for teaching and learning in the social studies. Unfortunately, children experience few opportunities to engage popular culture except outside of school. Even in the workplace, conversation often revolves around popular culture events. Why then do we avoid popular culture in the classroom?

Many schools have evolved into places where inquiry and active engagement are not encouraged. A standardized curriculum, instruction, and procedures dictate little risk taking. Teachers and administrators have become afraid to drift from the norm. Teachers often state they don't have time to integrate anything but the mandated curriculum. The accountability and achievement movement has severely limited what can occur in schools in the name of teaching and learning. A bland and boring social education has thus emerged (Hursh and Ross 2000).

Popular culture can counter this negative trend. If we are truly interested in kids being motivated to learn and apply this learning to the broader spectrum of social literacy, then we must make stronger efforts at integrating meaningful curriculum and instruction that includes real-world connections. These connections allow kids to develop the scaffolding needed to construct knowledge. Popular culture can enhance a transformative rather than transmissive social education by providing these connections.

MUSIC AS A TOOL FOR SOCIAL EFFICACY

Music is the universal language, or so the saying goes. Most people love music, which not only reflects culture and the times but functions as an active force in societal change. Music is a vital component of popular culture and the knowledge and understanding of popular music can be a powerful tool for developing social efficacy. Music is our students' preferred popular expression, even when compared to movies and television. It is essential for societal and cultural understanding. Yet, like other forms of popular culture, its role in schooling is minimal.

Music has tremendous global economic and cultural significance. It is situated both within international economics and industry and within personal social and even national identity (Shukar 1998). There is an increasing discourse regarding the influence and impact of popular music within academic circles and also in mainstream popular culture. Our students also deserve the opportunity to engage in this discourse and inquiry, for music is one area where they seem eager to share their voice and express social efficacy.

Unfortunately, music is seldom used in the teaching and learning process outside of traditional arts instruction. Traditional schooling is so entrenched with covering essential knowledge to ensure high test scores, that excuses are often used for not applying popular culture such as music. Teachers do not have enough time, popular music is inappropriate, it is not relevant, or there is just a lack of knowledge; all these are excuses for the lack of music integration in education. However, if we are interested in critical social efficacy for active participation and problem solving in society, then music offers many possibilities. And these excuses and issues must then be addressed.

ISSUES

Shuker (1994) suggests several issues regarding music and popular culture, including:

- Economic, market, and consumer issues related to music
- Cultural preferences and social factors
- Ideology, dominance, and agendas related to music
- Popular culture, music, and mass appeal
- Moral panic, popular culture, and music

These issues suggest a critical approach in using and analyzing music, much like that suggested in the popular efficacy movement. They should definitely be addressed, particularly as part of the promotion of critical social efficacy. A related issue is that these are often employed as reasons to belittle or demean popular music and popular culture as well, often leading to censorship and the like.

Economic, market, and consumer issues definitely affect the state of popular music. The issues of mass market and what sells often dictate kind and quality of music. Many even suggest that the idea of mass produced music for profit limits creativity and choice regarding music for the public. A few corporations dominate the music industry perhaps suggesting that these have become culture industries, creating our culture for us, less for creativity and pleasure sake than for corporate profits. The globalization of market ideals has often also created a global music market, often at the expense of the music and art in particular cultures (Negus 1992).

Related to the influence of corporations in music is the idea of cultural imperialism. Popular music as popular culture (at least in global sales) is dominated by the United States and Britain. As a result, global cultural preferences in music are often dominated by the top seller from the United States. Societal factors also influence popular music, which is perhaps the reason for the success of rap and hip-hop. Despite the power of the global music industry, class and ethnicity can often provide incredible influence on trends and even sales in popular music (Wallis and Malm 1992).

A particular critique of popular culture and music is the perceived ideology often inherent within in reinforcing dominant values and the agenda of those in power. Many suggest that what is popular only becomes accepted to ensure the status quo. In other words, the hegemonic powers would not allow much popular music to question or challenge entrenched societal values. Despite the perceived success of this agenda, much popular music has successfully usurped the system and affected societal change.

Popular culture and music as one vital component offer one of the few remaining avenues for common dialog and understanding. If nothing else, it often provides a context for connections to the world and sense making in the world. Passion and intrinsic appeal is somehow inherent in popular music and popular culture. This dialog and common understanding in popular music can be used to enhance critical social efficacy (White 1999).

Perhaps the more intriguing issue regarding popular culture and music is the idea of moral panic and the threat to society. As a result, new popular music is often subject to condemnation, censorship, and regulation. From the early experiences in pop such as Elvis to punk to heavy metal to hip-hop, music has been questioned regarding its legitimacy and impact on popular and society. Music is often viewed as promoting antisocial behavior and attitudes, and therefore many feel it must be controlled or at the very least ignored (Garofalo 1992). Thus popular music is rarely applied in schools as it is perceived to do little in meeting traditional goals. What one often finds in schools is a negative reaction to kid culture in whatever form (music, Pokemon, etc.) through stereotypes, banning, and demeaning acts and comments.

The baby boom generation contributed much to the mass audience for popular culture, and pop music reaped the benefits. One could provide an interesting social history of the latter half of the twentieth century by exploring the evolution of music. One initially finds the light-hearted bubble gum music of the 1950s and early 1960s that could represent the glory that was postwar America. As the 1960s progressed, music acquired a harder edge and explored social issues. The 1970s brought more self-indulgent music such as disco. In the late 1970s and 1980s punk, metal, and grunge explored serious issues once again. And in the 1990s hip-hop and alternative music pushed the boundaries and explored harder issues as well as entertained. Popular culture and music not only reflect the times can also be active social forces.

Economics also affects popular culture and music. Postwar prosperity enabled music to flourish as a dynamic force. Record, cassette, and now CD sales seemed to reach to new heights with every passing year. An essential component of popular culture is knowledge and awareness of music fads and trends. The economic climate of the times (whichever period one mentions) is again often reflected in the music (sound and lyrics) that is popular. Economic and social issues are particularly evident in the music of the late 1960s, early 1970s, early and late 1980s, and much of the

1990s. Economics within music can be investigated as an exciting social efficacy theme in the teaching and learning process.

Technology has also provided impetus for the development of music as popular culture and societal force. Incredible developments in the latter half of the twentieth century not only brought music to the masses but enabled innovative sounds and techniques to be introduced. Electric guitars, synthesizers, and computers have had a substantial impact of the evolution of music. Television, MTV, CDs, and the Internet can all be investigated regarding their influence on music, popular culture, and society. Technology has become a vital theme in society. Using technology as an agent in popular culture can facilitate the idea of social efficacy since technology and technology issues are so prevalent in today's society.

One of the most controversial issues related to the growth of music as popular culture is that of the influence of the music industry and the idea of corporate profits as the driving force for music. Central to the idea of popular culture is issue of business and popular music in the late twentieth century through today is nothing if not business driven. And this is the constant struggle. Artists often provide empowering social efficacy messages, but are also subject to personal sales. This often contradictory issue can provide much fodder for debate in the teaching and learning process. Issues related to capitalism, globalization, music choices, hegemony as the driving force, marketing, and how each relates to social efficacy could easily be integrated in schooling as we attempt to facilitate critical and active participation in society.

MUSIC AND EDUCATION

Much can be said concerning the possibilities of music in promoting critical social efficacy. And despite the lack of its use in schools, music has had a profound effect in popular culture as a force for social change. Instead of dismissing its potential, schools would be wise to work diligently on integrating popular music into the teaching and learning process if for no other reason than that there is a desperate need to improve the perceived relevance of schooling (at least in our kids' eyes).

There are a few instances of effective integration of music in schools. Obviously music programs help meet the needs of students into developing into more well-rounded human beings. An appreciation of music and art is vital for critical social efficacy, yet funding for the arts is the first to be cut in times of financial crisis. And now, with the emphasis increasingly placed on achievement of essential knowledge one often finds time for the arts being cut as well (Berliner and Biddle 1995).

There are also instances of teachers (mostly acting in isolation) who integrate music into their teaching environment. Some teachers play classical or jazz as background music as students work on assignments. Others allow students to bring in examples of their own to play during these assignment times, or even as free time sharing. Perhaps the most effective use is when a teacher integrates music into the teaching and learning process. Some social studies teachers, for example, have used music very effectively to demonstrate historical periods. Sample music integration examples include units on music and war, music and postwar America, the labor movement and music, social issues and music, and global cultures and music.

The learning is usually teacher directed, as the teachers choose and demonstrate the music examples. This is a first step in meaningful integration—modeling—but critical social efficacy necessitates more active student involvement and choice (Brooks and Brooks 1994). Critical social efficacy requires that we engage in a sincere effort at promoting the context and connections needed to ensure a more relevant learning experience. Allowing students to be involved in the social construction of meaning in their world is a vital step.

Keeping with social studies examples, using current events and social issues to provide context and connections for today and for the study of the past enhances the links necessary for student efficacy and empowerment. Popular music is a natural tool for achieving these goals. But it must be students' popular music. We can demonstrate ours as examples and modeling, but again, allowing students to include theirs in the teaching and learning process takes it that needed step. Only then can we hope to facilitate critical social efficacy.

Most music genres or individual artists include examples of songs that contain social commentary or historical references. Many people assume that social commentary in music reached its peak in the late 1960s and early 1970s. Punk, hip-hop, and grunge are genres from the 1980s through today that incorporate social commentary and historical references. And pop still has much to say regarding social efficacy. These genres are the ones that most interest our students. While we may not understand the music of today, we cannot become our parents and blindly dismiss its potential for critical social efficacy. Remember the early days of folk and rock.

MTV AND POPULAR MUSIC

MTV is one the most important popular culture influences of the times. MTV was a natural evolution of music and video as the world (and particularly the United States) became a television society. Children in the United

States and other nations had been brought up with television as an entertainment device and, in many instances a baby-sitter. The genius of MTV
was to tap into television and connect music (the common language of the
masses) with it through videos.

MTV has survived often justified criticism including racism and sexism. It
is yet another example of generational conflict and misunderstanding regarding popular culture and popular music. Despite this, MTV has had a
huge impact on popular culture, but also general society and culture. If
nothing else, television along with MTV has led many to recognize the
power and influence of popular culture.

MTV has influenced other aspects of popular culture too, such as movies,
television, and magazines. Many even suggest that it has influenced high
culture, including museums, theater, and classical music. This truly is the
MTV generation and we should allow for its use in teaching and learning
for critical social efficacy. Snippets of video can be used to great visual and
audio effect in critically analyzing social issues, for example. Music and
lyrics are one thing, but video can add yet another dimension for teaching
and learning.

Many forms of popular culture emerge as commentary or resistance toward mainstream culture and society. Perhaps no better example of this exists than in pop music. From its earliest days pop has been viewed as a cut-
ting-edge force, crossing boundaries and threatening the values and morals
of society. Little Richard, Elvis Presley, the Beatles, Bob Dylan, the Rolling
Stones, acid, heavy metal, disco, punk, MTV, grunge and thrash, rave, and
hip-hop have all had their detractors and have been viewed as threats to the
basic social fabric.

Through its history, pop, like all forms of popular culture, has served not
only as a reflection of the times but as a catalyst for critical social efficacy
and societal change. Several themes can be used to integrate pop music into
teaching and learning for social efficacy in schools. Pop music can be a
powerful theme as students investigate issues such as ethnicity and the
struggle for equality, population growth, economics, technology, business
and industry, efficacy and empowerment within the context of social history (Szatmary 2000). This focus provides the relevance students need to facilitate a love of learning leading to effective social efficacy.

Music in the United States in the last part of the twentieth century was often reflected through the struggle for equality by various ethnic groups, particularly African Americans. African American culture played a crucial role
in the history of popular music. Pop could not exist without the blues,
which originated in slave songs. Protest music of the 1960s often had civil
rights as the predominant theme. African American artists were trailblazers
in social commentary and music innovation, including blues, jazz, R&B,
disco, rap, and hip-hop. Each of these genres emerged as a proactive force

with music doing more than perhaps any other societal force in promoting integration and appreciation of cultures.

Perhaps the most relevant issue surrounding music (at least in regard to schooling) is its role as societal force, as this relates most directly to the issue of social efficacy. Regardless of the genre, popular music remains a vibrant cultural phenomena that reflects societal issues but can also have a proactive impact. Exploring the role of music in reflecting and impacting societal change can be a motivating experience for kids in their endeavor to make sense of the world. The idea that music not only supplies entertainment but also provides social commentary and perhaps even a call to arms for change makes it a powerful tool for social efficacy.

WHERE TO NOW?

Popular culture and social efficacy themes can make a difference for our children in their learning experience. The real question for us is, How can we remain complacent if we care about our children and their future? A society can only progress if it moves beyond transmission ideals and the status quo. We must recognize that the growing restrictions and accountability movements undermine participatory democracy. Harping on nonissues, prison and punishment mentality, the mythology of America as world savior, corporate and military welfare, and unbridled market globalization are antithetical to social justice. Creating a world of caring and compassion through social justice requires the cultivation of the human spirit, the nourishment of the imagination, and the impulse for self-expression (Purpel and Shapiro 1995).

We must not integrate popular culture for the sake of popular culture and to placate our troubled youth. We must provide opportunities for in-depth analysis of societal issues through popular culture, thus leading to social efficacy. We cannot ignore the issues regarding the economic and political factors possibly driving the choices we are given. The ideas of culture, culture icons, objectification, and social justice should be explored through in-depth inquiry, problem solving, and critical thinking. Using a Disney movie or a *Simpsons* episode just because the children like them is not enough.

Teachers and others interested in social efficacy and social justice approaches in schools must realize that neutrality is an impossibility. What is important is creating a classroom atmosphere where students and teachers are empowered to question and critically analyze social studies issues and themes. It is fine to disagree, but what is important is creating opportunities for students to act on their ideas (participate as citizens in our democracy). Popular culture embodies a language of both critique and possibility, a language that allows students to locate themselves in history, find their own voices, and establish convictions and compassion necessary for democratic civic courage (Freire and Giroux 1989). The concept of social efficacy is practically nonexistent in our country today. This should be our goal, through the integration of popular culture in teaching for social efficacy and social justice within the education process.

It is time to let the good times to roll in schools. Popular culture is an intrinsically motivating factor in our lives and should be integrated into the teaching and learning process in our schools. We are all very passionate about our likes and dislikes when it comes to popular culture. It can be a powerful tool as we hope to develop social efficacy within our students as it allows for transformative investigation. Allowing for the investigation of issues regarding popular culture as Shukar suggests (1994) or using it as social and historical references as Szatmary (2000) suggests can only enhance powerful teaching and learning that involves students in discourse and dialog. What better way to engage in critical inquiry and problem solving for social efficacy than to use popular culture within our schools!

REFERENCES

Berliner, D., and Biddle, B. (1995). *The manufactured crisis.* New York: Addison-Wesley.

Brooks, J., and Brooks, M. (1994). *The case for constructivist classrooms.* Alexandria, VA: Association for Supervision and Curriculum Development.

Chomsky, N. (2000). *Chomsky on mis-education.* Lanham, MD. Rowman & Littlefield.

Freire, P., and H. Giroux. (1989). Pedagogy, popular culture, and public life. In H. Giroux and R. Simon, eds., *Popular culture: Schooling and everyday life.* Granby, MA: Bergin & Garvey.

Garofalo, R., ed. (1992). *Popin' the boat: Mass music and mass movements.* Boston: South End.

Giroux, H. (1994). *Disturbing pleasures.* New York: Routledge.

Hursh, D., and Ross, E. W. (2000). *Democratic social education.* New York: Falmer.

Jennings, T. (1994). Social justice in the elementary classroom. *Social Studies and the Young Learner* 7(1): 4–6.

Loewen, J. (1995). *Lies my teacher told me.* New York: Touchstone.

Negus, K. (1992). *Producing pop: Culture and conflict in the popular music industry.* London: Edward Arnold. 1992.

Purpel, D., and S. Shapiro. (1995). *Beyond liberation and excellence.* Westport, CT: Bergin & Garvey.

Shuker, R. (1994). *Understanding popular music.* New York: Routledge.

——. (1998). *Key concepts in popular music.* New York: Routledge.

Steinberg, S., and J. Kincheloe. (1997). *Kinderculture: The corporate construction of childhood.* Boulder: Westview.

Szatmary, D. 2000. *Popin' in time: A social history of pop and roll.* Toronto: Prentice Hall, 2000.

Wallis, R., and Malm, K. *Popular Policy and Music Activity*. New York: Routledge. 1992.

Westheimer, J., and J. Kahne. (1998). Education for action: Preparing popular for participatory democracy. In William Ayers, Jean Ann Hunt, and Therese Quinn, eds., *Teaching for social justice*, 1–20. New York: New Press.

White, C. *Transforming social studies: A critical perspective*. Springfield, IL: Thomas, 1999.

2

The Spiderman Curriculum

Popular Culture in Social Studies

With great power there must also come—great responsibility.

—Stan Lee

We live in a media-saturated environment. Most of the images of the world around us (and how to make meaning of them) are established through popular media—television, film, video, magazines, posters, billboards, video games, the Internet. Each type of media not only gives messages but also suggests a way of understanding suggested by the media itself. Yet the power and pervasiveness of popular media are not acknowledged by many in education. Some teachers simply refuse to recognize the importance of popular culture in the lives of students. Rather, they see it as a distraction and pretend that they can fight the evil influence of popular culture by putting up posters like those sponsored by National TV-Turnoff Week and distributing stickers urging students to "kill your television set." Educators must accept that many of students' understandings about the world are constructed through popular culture texts.

Our students are constantly surrounded by an electronic environment that "literally 'bathes' them in digital media." They are confronted "continuously, during almost every waking hour, by multiple new forms of technological stimulation, from MTV to fast action films to the Internet, which was totally absent from previous generations" (Prensky 2001, 38). Based on the proliferation of electronic media, the mandate for popular culture, or media, literacy seems clear. As Postman (1985) has argued, popular culture rather than the classroom has become students' "first curriculum." Wishing that popular culture was not as pervasive and powerful as it is will not make it any less so.

The question facing educators is how to engage those texts meaningfully as part of the curriculum. Possibilities include more traditional methods of teaching through popular media texts (for entertainment, relevancy, or the perceived immediacy of experience) to engaging students to think critically about popular media texts. In the latter approach, teachers ask students to examine assumptions, attitudes, and values underlying the production, mediation, and consumption (especially students' own consumption) of such texts and how they position students to assume particular social, gendered, and racial reading positions (Ellsworth 1990) as they invite them to explore a constructed world in particular ways.

APPROACHES TO POPULAR CULTURE IN EDUCATION

Establishing that popular culture texts ought to be incorporated in the classroom is one thing. Determining how it might be done most effectively is another. Teachers must decide to what end(s) popular culture texts might be used with students? Three of the several options to consider are (1) popular culture as pedagogy; (2) popular culture for demystification, self defense, and social understanding; and (3) popular culture as a vehicle for critical and postmodern exploration. Given the transformative potential of social studies education, these classrooms seem a good fit for introducing students to the popular culture.

Popular Culture as Pedagogy

Social studies educators must recognize that most students find the lower-level memorization and recitation required in most social studies classes irrelevant and boring (Loewen 1995). Yet social studies can and should be exciting and involving. Teaching practices in the social studies should promote interest, engagement, rigor, enthusiasm for learning, and a sense of personal investment and empowerment. The use of popular cultural forms as a medium of pedagogy supports this goal.

In 1970, *Sesame Street* went on the air, illustrating how the teaching practices theorized above could look in practice. *Sesame Street* was an educational program based on a radical thought: if you can gain and hold the attention of children, they will learn. After decades, *Sesame Street* is still popular and obviously has been successful in holding children's attention. The show's secret—it is fun and entertaining (Prensky 2001). Unfortunately this is a conclusion that schools do not find relevant to the "business" of education. A common sentiment among administrators and other school officials is that schools are for work and not for fun. The idea of barring fun from the school day seems to be gaining momentum, compelled by the "north-bound high-stakes testing train." It is common knowledge that it is easier to get on board that train than it is to stand in front of it (Evans 2001; Grant 2001; Kohn 2000; McNeil 2000).

School is often unengaging for today's learners (Mahiri 2001; Gee 2003; Prensky 2001). Generally, when it comes to learning and teaching, educators care more about the content than they do about the learner. There is more concern over what to teach, rather than how or why. Prensky (2001) writes:

> people live in the world into which they are born, and do the things of their time that appeal to them. Because of the outside forces around them as they grew up, and because of normally living their early life in the last third of the twentieth century, learners' habits, preferences, and needs have radically changed. So, despite school's hundreds of years of 'tradition' it is now time for our education and training to finally change, or else to continue to fail us. Why? Because it no longer holds the interest of its students, even under duress. While there are many students who succeed at learning, in most places, they learn in spite of, not because of, their schools and training. (Prensky 2001, 68)

Teaching and learning can be more effective if students become emotionally connected with the information. Teachers can, through the use of popular culture, facilitate these emotional connections and thereby expedite the construction of meaning. This can be especially useful in social studies since students consider them the most irrelevant of all courses commonly found in schools (Loewen 1995). Loewen explains that "emotion is the glue that causes history to stick" (p. 294). Students can learn to associate important events in history with a particular song, singer, video, television show, actor/actress, or movie that was popular when the event occurred. One of the most often cited associations is from those people who remember where they were and what they were doing when they learned that President John F. Kennedy had been assassinated.

Social studies teachers who provide opportunities for students to create these emotional connections, through their incorporation of popular culture, will achieve the goal of powerful social studies teaching and learning. Using popular culture that is important in the lives of students in a classroom also gives them a chance for ownership, the "cornerstone of literacy education" (Shannon 1995, 23). It can provide a sense of authenticity, which, according to Shannon, is essential for literacy development: "Kids need to feel that what they are doing through language, they have chosen to do because it is useful or interesting or fun for them . . . What they do ought to matter to them personally" (p. 23).

While such an approach may be powerful, it does not necessarily mean it is meaningful. It might, in fact, work to popularize social studies education, even connect with students (not in any way insignificant achievements), while not necessarily promoting the goals of civic competence and education for democracy. As such, popular media become ends in themselves, rather than means to something else. They are used to seduce students to engage the traditional curriculum rather than as means to transform it. They are vehicles to pacify students rather than raise their critical engagement with such texts. Teaching is conducted *through* media rather than *about* media and the media remain transparent in the educative process. "As long as these sources of information are not subjected to critical scrutiny for their role as producers of knowledge," warns Masterman (1985), the prevailing views of media as natural and neutral conveyors of reality "will have been smuggled in under the guise of educational progressivism and relevance" (p. 65).

Popular Culture as Demystification, Self-Defense, and Social Understanding

Popular culture texts may also be used as curriculum. Educators ask students to deconstruct these texts in order to discover underlying truth and fallacies. Teachers sometimes ask students to identify popular culture that is important to them and then ask them to deconstruct it in order to discover "underlying truths" as a process of "demystification" (Buckingham 1998). According to Alvermann, Moon, and Hagood (1999), teachers adopt this demystification approach when they believe students are passively consuming popular culture: "So in an effort to educate them, the teacher assumes the role of a liberating guide for students who passively take in all forms of popular culture that surround them" (p. 25). It is often said that we need to learn to read between the lines in regard to media in order to understand what they are really about and to avoid being suckered. This is a common perspective on consumer culture according to Kenway and Bullen (2001):

> Consumer culture is seen variously to control, manipulate, segment and debase society, to contribute to the breakdown of local communities and to produce harmful forms of individualism and materialism. Some also suggest that it contributes to the bland cultural forms which cater to the lowest common denominator, thus undermining individuality and creativity. (Kenway and Bullen 2001, 14)

This perspective has roots in the Frankfurt School in the 1930s, particularly in the works of Adorno.

Following the Marxist model, Adorno (1991) argued that capitalism exploits people through the "culture industry," based on "the infantile compulsion towards the repetition of needs which it created in the first place"

(p. 58). Culture industries, according to Adorno, create, cultivate, and sat-
isfy their own false needs. These products are contrived to keep the masses
passively satisfied and politically apathetic: "The concoctions of the culture
industry are neither guides for a blissful life, nor a new art of moral responsibility, but rather exhortations to toe the line" (p. 91). The culture industry promotes a fetishism of commodity through advertising. As a result,
social relations and cultural experiences are objectified in terms of money.
We desire things because of how much they cost and "exchange value dis-
guise[s] itself as the object of enjoyment" (p. 34). The mass commercial culture, including popular media and music production, are characterized by
standardization, basically formulaic and similar: "the technique of the culture industry is, from the beginning, one of distribution and mechanical re-
production" (p. 87).

Baudrillard (1994) has similar views regarding the influence of popular
culture messages on the masses: "We are at a point in which information no
longer produces meaning, in fact it is the opposite that occurs" (p. 80). The
proliferation of media messages and the resulting implosion of meaning
cause individuals to cease their active involvement in socialization and to
mindlessly meld into a consumer group. For Baudrillard (1994), socialization is measured by the exposure to media messages. Social relations are
now formed in the sphere of consumption.

Baudrillard (1994) believed that consumer culture and television together "have produced an excess of images and signs which have led to a
world of simulation" (p. 15). This simulation, hyperreality, or Disneyfication has blurred the real and the imaginary to a point in which rediscover-
ing the real is no longer a possibility. The explosion of information in the
new media has led to an "implosion of meaning" (Baudrillard 1994, 81).
In this context, Kenway and Bullen (2001) explain that the "aestheticization
of reality" has led to "an endless flow of incongruous juxtapositions and to
a loss of referents, stable meanings and a sense of narrative, time and history" (p. 15). Once society gave meaning to images; now images give meaning to society.

Throughout history, social and cultural roles have often been defined by
consumer goods. According to Kenway and Bullen (2001), "people use
consumption to create identities, social bonds or distinctions and dis-
tances; to display and sustain differences; and to open or close off opportunities for themselves and for others" (p. 18). This tendency to make distinctions led to culture being defined as either high or low. *Experts* are a
potential by-product of high culture. This contributes to the perception
that high *art* is difficult, if not impossible, to understand. Conversely, experts cannot be produced through the interpretation of low culture, or
popular culture. The message in a work of popular culture is seemingly not

difficult to determine. As a result, popular culture often is dismissed as unimportant *fluff*, certainly not a serious enough topic for education to address. However, given its impact on all facets of life it should be taken seriously.

This might have been made even more important as schools have become complicit in the spread of consumer values. Sponsored educational materials (SEMs) are great temptations for beginning classroom teachers. Companies offer teachers free resources such as maps, videos, software, workbooks, posters, and so on. The catch is that all the materials contain advertisements for their sponsors. In 1995, *Consumer Reports* published *Captive Kids: A Report on Commercial Pressures on Kids at School,* which revealed nearly 80 percent of the SEMs they examined contained "biased or incomplete information in a way that favors the company or its economic agenda" (S.M. 1999). *The Nation* (September 27, 1999) included some examples of the "most-startling" SEMs from *Consumer Reports*. The first was a lesson plan and video called "Exxon: Scientists and the Alaska Oil Spill," that praises the efforts of the oil company in cleaning up the environment and wildlife in Alaska, while never revealing that they were the ones who caused the spill. Another example provided by *The Nation* was a nutrition guide called "The Chocolate Dream Machine," sponsored by Hershey, that discusses chocolate's place in a balanced diet. Since most SEMs are mailed directly to teachers, the burden then falls to them to become aware of the "hidden curriculum" inherent in most of these materials. As Trend (1995) writes, "Media are but a paper tiger—easily dismantled with the proper interpretative tools" (p. 9).

While SEMs are covertly influencing children in the schools, some marketing is more overt. Almost every school-related activity is influenced by corporations anxious to create new consumers: school buses carry advertisements, Coke and Pepsi create campus monopolies, and Channel One shows three minutes of advertising to students during class time. Barber (2000) believes that the "selling of students to corporations for the highest bid" is against all education is (or should be) about. This rampant commercialization in the schools

> violates the spirit of liberal education and contradicts the principles of any adequate pedagogy. Schools compelled by insufficient public funding (another consequence of privatization) are selling themselves and selling their students (that is, access to their students) in return for small donations from the corporate sector. (Barber 2000, 12)

Public education should be about creating critical thinkers and active capable citizens rather than passive consumers.

Cusic (2001) believes that popular culture must be examined in light of its potential effects in the economic realm. Advertising provides the majority of economic support for the entertainment industry. Newspapers, magazines, television, and radio sell time and space to advertisers, although there are other ways to influence consumption. Movies and television shows, especially those marketed to children, often encourage food and toy affiliations. Disney is probably the most obvious culprit in this regard. Giroux (1994) writes:

> The Wonderful World of Disney is more than a logo; it signifies how the terrain of popular culture has become central to commodifying memory and rewriting narratives of national identity and global expansion. Disney's power and its reach into popular culture combine an insouciant playfulness and the fantastic possibility of making childhood dreams come true—yet only through the reproduction of strict gender roles, and unexamined nationalism, and a notion of choice that is attached to the proliferation of commodities. (Giroux 1994, p. 31)

According to educators adhering to the "popular culture as demystification" approach, another commercial aspect of popular culture that students must realize is in the relatively new spheres of advertisement that can be found in movie product placements, sports product placements, and television "reality" shows. There are some very interesting examples of sports product placements that students can reflect on. For many years it has been the case that sports stars with sneaker endorsement contracts wear them on and off the court for the advertising benefit. The most provocative sports product placement must have been at the 1999 FIFA Women's World Cup, when Brandi Chastain took off her shirt to reveal her Nike sports bra. Ann Gerhart of the *Washington Post* reported that prior to the World Cup, Chastain had asked Nike to design a sports bra:

> On Saturday, when she ripped off her shirt in exultation after her World Cup-winning kick, the hard-bodied Chastain was wearing the sports bra she helped create. Nike is now drooling over its payday, rushing into production the new line it had planned to introduce at month's end and lining up promotional appearances for Chastain. (Gerhart 1999, C1)

In television, advertisement through product placement is not a new idea; however, the new reality show venues do seem to add a new dimension. NBC's recent reality show, *The Restaurant*, seems to be a juicier version of an infomercial. In addition to the traditional commercial spots, the show's corporate sponsors are all featured as a part of the show. In a technique referred to as "advertainment," customers are shown consuming cans of Coors Light, while the owner of the Restaurant is solving the problem of overdue payroll checks with his American Express card. The movie *Spiderman* (2002), aimed at the PG-13 age-group, featured at least fifteen national brand-name product placements.

The power and pervasiveness of popular culture makes it a force to be reckoned with. There is great potential for the artifacts of popular culture to render recipients into passive consumers and citizens. Popular culture has begun to replace the political in terms of shifting power from public to private (Kincheloe 2001; Barber 2000). There has been a transition from active to passive citizenship. The result of this power shift, according to Barber, is that "citizens become mere individuals, individuals become consumers, consumers become impulsive children" (p. 8). Barber also explains that children are ideal targets for popular culture because they are "innocent, impulsive, inexperienced, and capable of repetitive buying" (p. 12). However, since adults control the money, popular culture is marketed to the childish in adult consumers. Traditional adult values of "work, deferred gratification, saving, rationality, deliberateness (slowness), and complexity" are reorganized around infantilization (Barber 2000, 12). The new culture encourages values such as "play, impulse, consumption today, feeling, fastness (e.g., fast food), and simplicity" that are typical of children (Barber 2000, 12). Barber proposes that the new consumer values cause children to grow up faster so they can become consumers, "kidults," while, at the same time, adults are infantilized so they will behave like children and become "grown-downs rather than grown-ups" (Barber 2000, 12). Social studies educators have a crucial role to play in reclaiming and revitalizing an active citizenry. Social studies educators, following the demystification approach, recognize the influence of popular culture on political and/as social and economic consciousness (Kincheloe 2001) and work to actively engage such issues with their students.

Popular Culture Studies As Critical And Postmodern

A third approach for using popular culture in the classroom requires that educators understand and respect the "real" importance of popular culture in students' lives (Alvermann, Moon, and Hagood 1999; Buckingham 1998; Luke 1997). Educators recognize the expertise that students bring to the classroom and offer them several frameworks (drawn from feminism, postmodernism, and cultural studies) for examining popular culture texts. Using this combined, self-reflexive approach provides students the opportunity to protect their complex, at times contradictory individual readings of popular culture texts while still exploring the interplay of power, positionality, and subjectivity inherent in the production of those readings. This approach also encourages a multiplicity of interpretations as media texts are deconstructed. Students who are asked to read popular texts from these broader and multiple perspectives have the potential to develop a more powerful literacy to engage and explore popular culture texts (Alvermann, Moon, and Hagood 1999; Buckingham 1998; Ellsworth 1990; Luke 1994).

Teachers who adopt this approach ask students to go beyond merely analyzing popular media texts for demystification. Students are asked to investigate "how media and the mass-produced icons of popular culture situate us into relations of power by shaping our emotional, political, social, and material lives" (Luke and Roe 1993, 118). The purpose of this approach to critical media education should be to allow students to discuss the pleasures of popular culture, while also reading the texts from various perspectives. No truth or single reading is assumed. In his study of elementary-age students' readings of media texts, Buckingham (1998) found that students use their pleasures to examine their own understandings of the world and to develop new ones. This provides another challenge to educators since popular culture, as well as students' interactions with popular culture, are dynamic rather than static, and students can control and construct some of their experiences rather than serve as passive victims of media.

Empowering students to think critically has long been a rhetorical goal of schools. However, while schools do provide some educative activities aimed at developing critical thinking skills, they also act as agents of social control (Spring 1993). As Spring points out, the "use of knowledge as an instrument of power usually provokes political confrontation . . . Using education to enhance economic opportunities and increase political power also generates conflict" (p. 47). Even so, for several decades educators have been talking about the school's role in developing students' critical thinking skills. Most recently, the discourse regarding the needs of the "new economy" has described a growing demand for a new kind of worker who can problem-solve rather than blindly follow orders, ironically supporting the kind of thinking that contributes to engaged citizenship. Once again education remains mired in the traditional approach of transmitting knowledge rather than a more transformative approach to learning.

At present, our educational efforts are based on a modernist epistemological focus that offers certainty and definition. All knowledge to be transmitted lies in nice, neat categories of information that can be envisioned to be rather easily transmitted to our youth. The contemporary "back to basics" movement (certainly not the first one of these movements and, unfortunately, probably not the last) advocates limiting the focus of schools to essential knowledge and accountability through high-stakes testing. The role of schools, according to these advocates, is to inculcate traditional values in our youth. Within that educational paradigm is the concept of training students for the world of work in an industrial manufacturing economy that, for the most part, no longer exists. Yet schools today seem to most value (and reward) their students' punctuality and ability to sit silently and motionlessly for long periods of time. "Time on task" is one of the most important measures of a teacher's classroom effectiveness.

Empowerment and power, especially understanding how power functions, are the most important elements in critical literacy, especially that'since those who remain powerless are complicit in maintaining existing power relationships. Foucault (1990) explains, the idea of the circle of power:

> Power is everywhere; not because it embraces everything, but because it comes from everywhere . . . power is not an institution, and not a structure; neither is it a certain strength we are endowed with; it is the name that one attributes to a complex strategical situation in a particular society. (p. 93)

Foucault also believes that where there is power, there will always be resistance. However, the effectiveness of that resistance is based on the degree to which the powerless come to understand that power also comes from below and all sides, and that positions of power are fluid, shifting over time, place and experience.

The relatively *powerless, oppressed objects* in society must learn the importance of deconstructing the traditional current corporatized text of citizen. As Derrida states, deconstruction is justice (quoted in Spivak 1993). Power must be seen as productive, rather than merely repressive. Social injustice, social construction of knowledge, the nature of classroom culture, and the dissolution of identities are important concerns in reconceptualizing the schools' role in the contemporary power paradigm (McLaren and Gutierrez 1994). Schools must become places where all voices are heard and where people learn to recognize power structures and negotiate power arrangements.

Educators must also develop critical thinking skills among students, in order to combat the trend of abandonment of active citizenship for passive consumerism. It is imperative that this shift from public power to private power be ameliorated. In order to be able to make the informed decisions that will be required of them in the future by active citizenship, students must be taught to question how their identities are constructed by popular culture.

Social studies educators, Kincheloe (2001) explains, need to understand that the purveyances of popular culture often inadvertently further a variety of social and/or cultural agendas. He cites the example of the *Home Alone* (1990, 1992) movies as evidence of how right-wing cultural politics vilifies women. There are many other productions that affect the constructions of our social, cultural, economic, and political consciousness. Those who adopt passive consumer roles will therefore be rejecting active citizenship. Teachers must provide students the opportunities to explore "how media and the mass-produced icons of popular culture situate us into relations of power by shaping our emotional, political, social, and material lives (Luke and Roe 1993, 118).

According to Kincheloe (2001), the powerful and prolific nature of popular culture has significantly expanded the realm of social studies: "Racial and gender issues are only a couple of the numerous areas addressed in this media/popular culture-based social studies curriculum of the contemporary era" (p. 12). Social studies must provide students the tools (literacies) with which to read the world. Students must question the way their identities have been shaped by popular culture: "Every movie, every textbook, and every magazine addresses an ideal audience that is most often defined in terms of a national collectivity. This interpellation is so ubiquitous that is seems nonexistent. It is simply assumed" (Trend 1995, 36–37).

Ellsworth (1990) explained that certain films "structure and mobilize signs and meanings circulating within the culture in a way that offers viewers a social place to stand within that structure" (p. 14). According to Ellsworth, the "telling of the story encourages us to identify with some of the characters and their points of view, desires, experiences, relations with other characters" (p. 15). Therefore, in order to make sense of a film,

> the viewer must be able to adopt—if only imaginatively and temporarily—the social, political, and ideological interests that are the conditions for the knowledge it constructs. In this way the film's discourse seeks to engage the viewer not only in the activity of knowledge construction, but in the construction of knowledge from a particular social, political, and ideological point of view. Thus, "viewing experience" must be seen not as voluntary and idiosyncratic, but as fundamentally relational—a projection of particular kinds of relations between self, others, knowledge, and power. (Ellsworth 1990, 13)

Children can be taught to use media for their own ends by actively interpreting how media function and learning how to read them. That is, just as children have been taught to read for meaning, they can be taught to make meaning from media as well.

Giroux (1997) calls for a pedagogy that provides "the terrain through which students critically engage and challenge the diverse cultural discourses, practices and popular media they experience in their everyday existence" (p. 234). It is critical that students appreciate that the power of mass media, "with its massive apparatuses of representation and its mediation of knowledge—is central to understanding how the dynamics of power, privilege, and social desire structure the daily life of a society" (Giroux 1997, 235). One of the most powerful media giants influencing children's culture is the Walt Disney Company. Giroux (1994) believes that the "cultural texts that dominate children's culture, including Disney's animated films should be incorporated into schools as serious objects of social knowledge and critical analysis" (p. 10).

Interestingly, he supports using Disney's animated films intact: "[Films] should be neither ignored nor censored by those who dismiss the conservative ideologies they produce and circulate" (p. 10). He then calls for parents, educators, and others to find ways to make Disney accountable for what it produces (p. 13). While Giroux (1994) criticizes Disney for its conservative approach to issues, the Ethics and Religious Liberty Commission (ERLC) of the Southern Baptist Convention has developed criticisms of the exact opposite nature against Disney. In 1997, CNN Online reported that the leaders of the Southern Baptist Convention voted to endorse a boycott of all things Disney (www.cnn.com/US/9706/18/baptists/disney). They once referred to their website as Your Official Disney Boycott Site! On that site they had listed "twenty-three reasons (and counting) to beware of the 'Magic Kingdom.'" According to the page's authors, "The Disney Company has the potential to do much good, and it has. Likewise, Disney also has the power to do enormous harm—and it has" (www.erlc.com/Culture/Disney/ 1997/case.htm). The ERLC does not cite any of the good but has a wide variety of the bad. Some examples are: glorified pagan earth worship in Pocahontas (1995), smeared the president's reputation in Jefferson in Paris (1995) (the Sally Hemings allegations), and the pro-homosexual agenda of Disney in general (particularly Disney-owned Hyperion Press). The irony is that Disney is vilified by conservatives for being too liberal and by liberals for being too conservative.

Educators must provide students with the tools to critically analyze how the texts from Disney and other media purveyors are constructed and construct viewers. Students become empowered and are then capable of transforming themselves from objects to subjects, from passive to active (Giroux 1994; Kellner 1995). By learning to read texts from a variety of viewpoints, students can develop literacies that value difference, and can use the awareness of difference in creating a moral vision that a single perspective can never offer: "Our abilities to mediate dominant readings and spectator positionings can be improved with study and . . . these skills can be taught to children regardless of age or grade level" (Trend 1995, 33).

CONCLUSION

Popular culture, now the dominant form of culture, provides many of the texts through which students gain identity and socialization. There are several ways that social studies educators might address the powerful nature of popular culture. One is to consider popular culture as a vehicle for pedagogy. In this approach, educators attempt to connect with students who feel unchallenged and unengaged by classes that emphasize content coverage rather than meaningful learning opportunities. A second approach to incorporating popular culture in the classroom emphasizes its role in demystification, self-defense, and social understanding. Educators use popular culture texts as targets for analysis. This approach disregards any pleasure the students received from the popular culture texts being analyzed and tends not to acknowledge multiple interpretations. A more self-reflexive approach that acknowledges both the students' expertise in, and the pleasure derived from, popular culture is the critical and postmodern approach. It is important to note that this sort of pedagogy for cultural, critical literacy should be constructed with, not for all people (Gore 1993, 120). Popular media literacy would allow students to learn that culture goes well beyond the one dimensional picture of America that is limited and reinforced by the most popular cultural texts (Giroux 1994; Kellner 1995; Trend 1995). Students are given the opportunity to read these texts from their own perspective, as well as from peers and teachers and from other perspectives such as feminism, postmodernism, and cultural studies. Critical media literacy also requires abandoning assumptions that particular readings are self-evident or that a medium itself is a neutral carrier of information. Students must develop literacy skills to be able to decode the symbols, or signs (the semiotic meaning) attached to those texts.

REFERENCES

Adorno, T. (1991). *The culture industry: Selected essays on mass culture*. London: Routledge.

Alvermann, D., Moon, J., Hagood, M. (1999). *Popular culture in the classroom: Teaching and research critical media literacy*. Newark, DE: International Reading Association.

Barber, B. (2000). Challenges to the common good in the age of globalism. *Social Education* 64(1): 8–13.

Baudrillard, J. (1994). *Simulacra and simulation*. Trans. S. Glaser. Ann Arbor: University of Michigan Press.

Buckingham, D., ed. (1998). *Teaching popular culture: Beyond radical pedagogy*. London: University College/London Press

Cusic, D. (2001). The popular culture economy. *Journal of Popular Culture* 35(3): 1–10.

Ellsworth, E. (1990). Educational film against critical pedagogy. In E. Ellsworth and M. Whatley, eds., *The ideology of images in educational media: The hidden curriculum in the classroom*, 10–26. New York: Teacher College Press.

Ethics and Religious Liberty Commission of the Southern Baptist Connection. www.erlc.com.

Evans, R. (2001). Thoughts on redirecting a runaway train: A critique of the standards movement. *Theory and Research in Social Education* 29(2): 330–339.

Foucault, M. (1990). *The history of sexuality*. Vol. 1, An introduction. Trans. R. Hurley. New York: Vintage.

Gee, J. (2003). *What video games have to teach us about learning and literacy*. New York: Palgrave.

Gerhart, A. (1999). Chastain lifts sports apparel market. *Washington Post*, July 14, C1.

Giroux, H. (1997). Is there a place for cultural studies in colleges of education? In H. Giroux and P. Shannon, eds., *Education and cultural studies: Toward a performative practice*, 231–47. New York: Routledge.

———. (1994). *Disturbing pleasures: Learning popular culture*. New York: Routledge.

Gore, J. (1993). *The struggle for pedagogies: Critical and feminist discourses as regimes of truth*. New York: Routledge.

Grant, S. (2001). An uncertain level: Exploring the influence of state-level testing in New York State on teaching social studies. *Teachers College Record 103*(3): 398–426.

Jefferson in Paris. (1995). Dir. J. Ivory. Burbank, CA: Touchstone Pictures.

Kellner, D. (1995). *Media culture: Cultural studies, identity, and politics between the modern and the postmodern*. London: Routledge.

Kenway, J., and Bullen, E. (2001). *Consuming children: Education, entertainment, advertising*. Buckingham, England, UK: Open University Press.

Kincheloe, J. (2001). *Getting beyond the facts: Teaching social studies/social sciences in the twenty-first century*. New York: Lang.

Kohn, A. (2000). Burnt at the high stakes. *Journal of Teacher Education 51*(4): 315–327.

Loewen, J. (1995). *Lies my teacher told me: Everything your American history textbook got wrong*. New York: New Press.

Luke, C. (1997). Media literacy and cultural studies. In S. Muspratt, A Luke, and P. Freebody, eds., *Constructing critical literacies: Teaching and learning textual practice*, 19–49. Cresskill, NJ: Hampton.

Luke, C. (1994). Feminist pedagogy and critical media literacy. *Journal of Communication Inquiry 18*(2): 30–47.

Luke, C., and Roe, K. (1993). Introduction to special issues: Media and popular culture studies in the classroom. *Australian Journal of Education 37*: 115–118.

M., S. (1999). The corporate curriculum. *The Nation*, September 27 1999, 17.

Mahiri, J. (2001). Pop culture pedagogy and the end(s) of school. *Journal of Adolescent and Adult Literacy 44*(4): 382–85.

Masterman, L. (1985). *Teaching the media*. London: Comedia.

McLaren, P., and Gutierrez, K. (1994). Pedagogies of dissent and transformation. *Journal of Educational Reform 3*(3): 327–37.

McNeil, L. (2000). *Contradictions of school reform: Educational costs of standardized testing*. New York: Routledge.

Pentecost, J. (Producer), and Gabriel, M. (Director). (1995). *Pocahontas* [Motion Picture]. Burbank, CA: Watt Disney Pictures.

Postman, N. (1985). *Amusing ourselves to death: Public discourse in the age of show business*. New York: Penguin.

Prensky, M. (2001). *Digital game-based learning*. New York: McGraw-Hill.

Shannon, P. (1995). *Text, lies, and video tape: Stories about life, literacy, and learning*. Portsmouth, NH: Heinemann.

Spiderman. (2002). Dir. S. Raimi. Culver City, CA: Columbia Pictures.

Spivak, G. (1993). *Outside in the teaching machine*. New York: Routledge.

Spring, J. (1993). *Conflict of interests: The politics of American education*. White Plains, NY: Longman.

Trend, D. (1995). *The crisis of meaning in culture and education*. Minneapolis: University of Minnesota Press.

3

Critical Media Literacy

It has become quite popular to bemoan the loss of innocence in today's youth and the role that popular culture has played in their demise. Society today is facing some serious, complicated problems and it becomes very easy to lay the blame for our societal ills at the foot of a group of activities that is the major source of entertainment and communication for today's youth. Unfortunately this is overly simplistic and, by devaluing the interests of today's children, it runs the risk of further alienating our younger generations. This chapter seeks to provide a brief description of the relationship between today's youth, popular culture and society; provide a case for the importance of diversity in the varying forms of popular culture; and suggest how media literacy programs can prepare today's youth to actively create more diverse and representational content in popular culture.

YOUTH, SOCIETY, AND POPULAR CULTURE: AN OPPOSITIONAL RELATIONSHIP

Popular culture is a reflection of the masses. It is a basic commonality that ties people together. The stories of popular culture were once told by wandering minstrels around campfires and were passed down from generation to generation by the tribal or family elders. With the advent of silent movies in the 1920s, radio in the 1940s, rock and roll in the 1950s, television and now the Internet, the mode of popular culture and storytelling has changed. As the means of popular culture changed, some remained nostalgic for the past, fondly remembering their youth and wanting to recreate it for their children. As adults they try to restore the popular culture that was familiar to them and as a result the popular culture created by the next generation sometimes becomes a source of fear and concern; the cultural gap, in fact, is a generation gap (McDonnell 1994).

The debate over the value and lasting effects of the different modalities of popular culture has changed little over the past eighty years. As was true with new modalities of popular culture in the past, in some settings, it is the mark of a literate and cultured person to criticize television and other forms of popular media. Although now viewed as benign, the *Nancy Drew* and *Hardy Boys* series were a source of concern and debate in the middle part of the twentieth century for their ability to confuse fantasy with reality, cause children to question authority, and encourage children to abandon real literature (McDonnell 1994). This concern seems to reflect a belief that childhood is primarily a preparation and training for adulthood and as a result much of what is kids' popular culture would serve little benefit. This presumes that all children's pursuits should have an elevated purpose, a standard that adults do not apply to their own entertainment. Popular culture represents an opportunity for children to have fun and express themselves. The popularity of Robert Munsch books, anime, and *The Simpsons* television show reflects a need for children to exert control and power (McDonnell 1994). Through these characters and stories children are able to express anger and rebelliousness that they are not regularly permitted to reveal. There is a growing concern that the dismissal and denunciation of youth popular culture is symptomatic of a societal pessimism toward the future that is projected onto youth. Consequently schools resemble prisons and young people are feared; in fact youth has "no standing in the public sphere" (Giroux 2003).

For decades a debate has raged on the effect of the increasing violence in television, movies, and video games. Integral to these debates is the question of what constitutes a violent act. There is often no distinction made between incidents in comedies, dramas, cartoons, and live action. While exposure to episodes of violence in modes of popular culture may appear to be an obvious source of rising violence in our society, it is an explanation that denies the complexity of the social ills of our times. Children with more aggressive behavior (and therefore more prone to violence) come from families where the parents are very authoritarian, use physical punishment, have heavy television viewing habits, and the children engage in less fantasy play. Research also indicates that children who are able to use fantasy play to assimilate the experiences they are exposed to are less likely to become violent. Another concern of adults is that children will become desensitized to violence, whereas the research seems to indicate that children become desensitized to television violence, which they understand is not real (McDonnell 1994).

Much has been written on the negative effects of the isolating, solitary qualities of the modes of popular culture and their use. Societal changes of the past twenty-five years have created a generation of teenagers who feel isolated and lacking in a sense of community. Technology and television fill in that void and become their chosen method of communication and information about the world. John Katz, an author and media critic quoted in an article for *Educational Leadership*, said that "technology is youth culture" (Tell 1999). Students do not view technology as a set of skills to be acquired to perform tasks or perfected for future work. Technology is how they communicate. McDonnell said it best when she suggested that "we do more than just censor and rage . . . We must understand and embrace the wild, anarchic character" of kids' popular culture (McDonnell 1994, 20).

In an increasingly fragmented, technology-driven world, popular culture teaches us how to survive, unfortunately at a high cost—consumerism (McDonnell 1994). It cannot be denied that popular culture contains negative messages embedded within about the dominance of males and Western European ideas. While popular culture is part of the reality of the masses, it is important to remember that it is individuals who are taking in the messages and creating meaning. Popular culture can potentially provide a forum for the development of critical media literacy in our students; by recognizing the political, social, and cultural aspects of media literacy a true multiculturalism built on alliances, "freedom, liberation, democracy and critical citizenship" could exist in our schools (McLaren 1995, 107).

THE IMPORTANCE OF DIVERSITY IN POPULAR CULTURE TO PROMOTE INCLUSION

Media brings the world into our homes. From them, we learn about war and peace, the environment, new scientific discoveries, and so on. We are dependent upon mass communication for knowing what is going on in our physical, social, economic, and political environments. In other words, almost everything we know about people, places, and events, which we cannot visit firsthand, comes from the media. We also rely on media for entertainment and pleasure. Television and film have become the storytellers of our generation: these stories tell us about who we are, what we believe, and what we want to be. (Tyner 2003)

Since it is clear that students are learning about the world and themselves through media, the issues of diversity and how well what they see represents themselves become important. Children have also identified the importance of seeing diversity in programming; children felt that diverse television programming (Media Now 2002):

- Tells children that people of their race are important (84 percent)
- Makes children of that race feel included (81 percent)
- Provides role models (78 percent)

Most developmental theories tell us that children learn about themselves and others simply by observing those around them. This learning takes place in the context of their personal needs, interests, skills, and inducements. So time spent in front of the television becomes a significant learning activity (Media Now 2002). When stereotypical images like the Hispanic maid, the African American housekeeper, or uneducated immigrant are all that is seen the effect on an individual's self image can be very negative. In light of the proliferation of American media both here and abroad, the program content becomes a global concern. The depiction of different cultures and peoples as well as the roles they play in the shows represents to the viewer an attitude toward a people. In this way American television tells the people of the world what we think of them.

In order to clarify ideas on multiculturalism, it maybe helpful to identify three common attitudes; I found the distinctions made by McLaren (1995) very useful. He identifies three major attitudes toward multiculturalism. First, conservative multiculturalism is described best in terms of colonial attitudes, manifest destiny, imperialism, and the portrayal of nonwhite Europeans as slaves or servants. Languages and dialect are deemphasized in a push towards a common culture. Unsuccessful minorities result from cultural deprivation or a lack of family and values. To be white is not an ethnicity but the standard. Second, liberal multiculturalists feel that a cognitive and social equality exists between the races but a current lack of educational and social opportunity has created a situation of inequality. While this position holds the promise of reform, it tends to become ethnocentric and centers on Anglo-American norms. Third, the left liberal view of multiculturalism is all about defining difference. To gain credibility within society one must be closely aligned with an oppressed people. Difference becomes significant in that it creates an identity. From this perspective "exists an authentic female or African American or Latino experience" (McLaren 1995, 97). The problem with all three of these perspectives is that there remains a dominant social order and that ideas of either sameness (conservative or liberal) or difference (left-liberal) define individual identities (McLaren 1995). Instead what is needed is what can be defined as critical and resistance multiculturalism, a term that is borrowed from McLaren (1995), but its elements can also be found in the works of Giroux (1997), Loewen (1995), Percoco (2001), and Spring (2004). Critical and resistance multiculturalism is centered on the idea that diversity should be acknowledged and that conflicts build cultures and democracies. By acknowledging differences we can better understand the history, culture, power, and ideology which produced them. It is away from the old ideas and toward this new attitude concerning multiculturalism that educators should direct students. Furthermore, if this new attitude is not incorporated into the major source of news and entertainment for young people, then it becomes a schoolhouse exercise that has no relevance in the culture in which students live.

MEDIA LITERACY: TEACHING STUDENTS TO ACTIVELY PURSUE DIVERSITY IN MEDIA

Information is the "black gold" of this generation and many people do not know where they "are going on the information highway . . . they just live life on the road" (Barber 1996, 101). The Internet, along with television and movies, is making an increasing amount of information available at a rate that increases in both quantity and speed exponentially. With youth's growing reliance on all types of media for communication, it becomes the concern of educators to teach students to be aware of the messages they view everyday. Time made "You" its person of the year in 2006 what with Youtube, MySpace, and other sites so popular among youth. Nevertheless, it is not enough to merely understand and analyze the information presented; students should also be empowered to affect change. A critical media literacy practice can be used to transform the messages sent through the media to support an emancipatory democracy, one that reflects a critical and resistance multiculturalism. Barber (1996) notes that television is Americanizing the world at an alarmingly fast rate. He observes that while churches are unique to a region, movie theaters are similar throughout the world. It is with some sarcasm that he quotes Bill Roedy, European director of MTV, who gives partial credit to MTV for the democratization of East Germany as it allowed a more "free flow of information and expression" which opened a "window on the rest of the world" (Barber 1996, 108). While there is no way to prove or disprove Roedy's claim, any culture that relies on instant pictures and news blurbs jeopardizes deliberative, democratic debate and discussion (Barber 1996). In a world where one picture can produce or change governmental policy it becomes crucial to teach and remind students of the importance of public debate and deliberate decision making despite the tendency toward fast-paced reactionary attitudes.

In the past media literacy focused on two basic skills bases. One is in the area of cognitive thinking skills. Media literacy programs designed with this framework in mind taught students to scrutinize and observe media. Programs are viewed and then discussed with the goal of finding meaning. The student remains largely passive in this context (Sholle and Denski 1995). One example of an approach like this is the outline offered by the Media Awareness Network (n.d.).

1. Help students become aware of and manage their television diet.
2. Learn skills to become critical viewers of television.

3. Teach students to explore the deeper issues like; who benefits from the media, who is excluded and why.

A second area of focus for media literacy programs was in the area of visual skills. Students are taught to view programs with a discriminating eye. They are able to distinguish good and bad programming as well as judge political correctness (Sholle and Denski 1995). A third more powerful course is the critical media literacy approach advocated by Sholle and Denski (1995), McLaren (1995), and Giroux (1997), and acknowledges a complex political, social, and cultural practice. It seeks to cause debate and discussion. By its very nature it concerns itself with culture and power. By using a critical media literacy approach, we can build powerful learners and citizens who are able to ask the critical questions needed to understand the information presented to them. These authors identify three important components of a highly effective critical media literacy program:

1. Students should examine media presentations for hidden meanings.
2. Students should critically examine their reasons for choosing the media that they do.
3. Students should engage in reading, writing, and active transformation of the system.
4. Students should see that the future holds opportunities for expression and unity.

Barber (1996) echoes this sentiment when he suggests that we use the media for more civic interests and subjects. The current trends toward a vertical and horizontal integration of the print media, movies, and television put at risk the public conversations he supports.

While popular culture provides a foundation for student's experiences, it should not be criticized or accepted without criticism (Sholle and Denski 1995). Through the process of implementing the language and activities of critical media literacy, students can transform their preferred modes of entertainment and communication to better reflect themselves and those around them. Through this forum students can begin to build hope in the future. As the media reflects those who view it in a more accurate and balance way then discussions on citizenship, democracy and justice are more likely to be productive. Giroux (2003) is not alone in his fear that today's youth is being disenfranchised: a process of critical media literacy can stop that progression. A more diverse media will build community and allow all of us to actively affect much need social change.

REFERENCES

Barber, B. R. (1996). *Jihad vs. McWorld: How globalism and tribalism are reshaping the world.* New York : Ballantine.

Giroux, H. A. (1997). Is there a place for cultural studies in colleges of education? In H. A. Giroux and P. Shannon, eds., *Educational and cultural studies towards a performative practice,* 231–47. New York : Routledge.

———. (2003). *The abandoned generation democracy beyond the culture of fear.* New York: Palgrave Macmillian.

Loewen, J. W. (1995). *Lies my teacher told me: Everything your American history textbook got wrong.* New York: Simon & Schuster.

McDonnell, K. (1994). *Kid culture: Children and adults and popular culture.* Toronto, Ont.: Second Story.

McLaren, P. (1995). White terror and oppositional agency: Towards a critical multiculturalism. In P. McLaren, R. Hammer, D. Sholle, and S. Reilley, eds., *Rethinking media literacy: A critical pedagogy of representation,* 87–124. New York: Lang.

Media Awareness Network. (2003). What is media literacy? www.media-awareness.ca/english/teachers/media_literacy/index.cfm.

Media Now. (2002) Why it matters: Diversity on television. www.childrennow.org/media/medianow/mnsummer2002.htm.

Percoco, J. A. (2001). *Divided we stand: Teaching about conflict in U.S. history.* Portsmouth, NH: Heinemann.

Sholle, D., and Denski, S. (1995). Critical media literacy: Reading, remapping, and rewriting. In P. McLaren, R. Hammer, D. Sholle, and S. Reilley, eds., *Rethinking media literacy: A critical pedagogy of representation,* 6–31. New York: Lang.

Spring, J. (2004). *Deculturalization and the struggle for equality.* New York: McGraw-Hill.

Tell, C. (1999). Generation what? Connecting with today's youth. *Educational Leadership,* December, 8.

Tyner, K. (2003). Why teach media literacy? www.media-awareness.ca/english/teachers/media_literacy/index.cfm.

4

American Idiots?

Current U.S. Protest Music and Social Activism

Is there vibrant protest music in the United States today that leads to social activism? Many bemoan what they consider the dearth of socially relevant music today. Critique ranges from marketing, the next new band, or a continued bombardment of sound and image. Despite this harking back to the grand old protest days of the 1960s and early 1970s when one heard Bob Dylan, Joan Baez, Marvin Gaye, Buffalo Springfield, and others on mainstream radio, much can be said about protest music today. We all seem to prefer our popular culture icons. My son's name is Dylan. Perhaps this dismissal and, yes, ignorance of current music is a sign of the times. Music does seem to be all over the place; and there are points to be made regarding the issue of it all being about marketing. We are in the age of Clear Channel after all.

The growth of socially relevant music that leads to increased involvement and activism is an outcome of a variety of recent events including the Bush presidency, 9/11, the war in Iraq, the perceived role of the United States in the world and issues related to social justice. Current examples include moveon.org's activity regarding music as a social force (Future Soundtrack for America and the Vote for Change Tour), Rock Against Bush CDs, soundtracks from documentaries such as *Fahrenheit 911*, and numerous individual artists writing music focusing on social commentary (Eminem, U2, Michael Franti, Ani Defranco, Green Day, Rise Against, System of a Down). Issues discussed will include the role of artists in social change, music and marketing/capitalism, music and activism, and music and societal change. The following discussion will analyze current protest music as a societal force.

MUSIC AND POPULAR CULTURE

What is the role of protest music in society? Is there a connection between popular culture, protest music, and social efficacy and activism? Popular culture is at the center of societal controversy and debate at present. Many from one end of the spectrum criticize its very nature and suggest that it only serves to destroy American morals and values. These folks call for increased censorship and the like. Many on the other end of the spectrum also criticize the nature of popular culture and suggest that it only perpetuates the status quo and enhances corporate and American hegemony. These folks call for more openness and less corporate domination of our culture.

We do need to acknowledge that popular culture is part of our lives and is very important to our society, our citizens, and especially our children, regardless of the debate or which spectrum one subscribes to. In a society increasingly fragmented by debate, misunderstandings, and lack of consensus, perhaps popular culture remains one of the few arenas that provides a forum for common understandings, dialog, and communication. It is precisely in the diverse spaces and spheres of popular culture that most of the education and social efficacy that matters today is taking place on a global scale (Giroux 1994).

What is the connection we all seem to have with pop culture? As stated earlier, popular culture is rife with controversy and currently receives strong criticism from all areas of the political spectrum. Much of the criticism is warranted; yet despite political leanings there seems to be some general agreement regarding the underlying problems with media culture and its impact on society and especially our children. Neither simplistic generalizations calling for censorship nor attempts at ignoring the influence of media culture are needed.

Popular culture has never been so dominant in our lives, yet it is experiencing incredible criticism. Many are at a loss at how to deal with its influences. A strong argument can be made that pop culture has become the most influential education institution for our children in society, and many seem quite frustrated by this. Rather than fight to ensure one's own agenda in popular culture, it might be better to use it as an opportunity to promote social efficacy and activism.

Our society has made pop culture a cornerstone of cultural identity and we simply cannot ignore that fact. Music, television, movies, and other media provide fodder for connections among our disconnected citizenry. Why not use this, rather than belittle it?

Music is the universal language, or so the saying goes. Most people love music. It is not only a reflection of culture and the times, but it is also often an active force in societal change. Music is a vital component of popular culture and the knowledge and understanding of music can be a powerful tool for developing social efficacy and activism. It is vital for societal and cultural understanding.

Music has tremendous global economic and cultural significance. It is situated both within international economics and industry and within personal social and even national identity (Shukar 1998). There is an increasing discourse regarding the influence and impact of popular culture and music within academic circles and also in mainstream media. We all deserve the opportunity to engage in this discourse and inquiry for music is one area where they seem eager to share their voice and express social efficacy.

However, if we are interested in critical social efficacy for active participation and problem solving in society, then music offers many possibilities. And these excuses and issues must then be addressed.

ISSUES

Shuker (1994) suggests several issues regarding music and popular culture:

- Economic, market, and consumer issues related to music
- Cultural preferences and social factors
- Ideology, dominance, and agendas related to music
- Media culture, music, and mass appeal
- Moral panic, media culture, and music

These issues suggest a critical approach in using and analyzing music, much like that suggested in the media literacy movement. They should definitely be addressed, particularly as part of the promotion of critical social efficacy and activism. A related issue is that these are often employed as reasons to belittle or demean media music and media culture as well, often leading to censorship.

Economic, market, and consumer issues affect the state of media music. The issues of mass market and "what sells" often dictate kind and quality of music. Many even suggest that the idea of mass-produced music for profit limits creativity and choice regarding music for the public. A few corporations dominate the music industry, perhaps suggesting that these have become culture industries, creating our culture for us, less for creativity and pleasure than for corporate profits. The globalization of "market ideals" has often also created a global music market, often at the expense of the music and art in particular cultures (Negus 1992).

Related to the influence of corporation in music is the idea of cultural imperialism. Music as popular culture (at least in global sales) is dominated by the United States and Britain. As a result, global cultural preferences in music are often dominated by the top seller from the United States, for example. Societal factors also influence media music, which is perhaps the reason for the success of rap and hip-hop. Despite the power of the global music industry, class and ethnicity can strongly influence trends and even sales in media music (Wallis and Malm 1992).

A particular critique of popular culture and music is the perceived ideology often inherent within in reinforcing dominant values and the agenda of those in power. Many suggest that media only become accepted to ensure the status quo. In other words, the hegemonic powers would not allow much media music to question or challenge entrenched societal values. Despite the perceived success of this agenda, much media music has successfully usurped the system and affected societal change.

Popular culture and especially music are vital components and, as noted earlier, few of the remaining avenues for possible common dialog and understanding. If nothing else, they often provide a context for connections to the world and sense making in the world. Passion and intrinsic appeal are somehow inherent in media music and media culture. This dialog and common understanding in media music can be used to enhance critical social efficacy (White 1999).

Perhaps the more intriguing issue regarding pop culture and music is the idea of moral panic and threat to society. As a result, music is often subject to condemnation, censorship, and regulation. From the early experiences in pop such as Elvis to punk to heavy metal to hip-hop, music has been questioned regarding its legitimacy and impact on media and society. Music is often viewed as promoting antisocial behavior and attitudes in media; therefore many feel it must be controlled or at the very least ignored (Garofalo 1992).

The baby boom generation born after World War II contributed much to the mass audience for media culture and therefore music; and pop music in all its categories reaped the benefits. One could provide an interesting social history of the latter half of the twentieth century by exploring the evolution of music. One initially finds the lighthearted bubble gum music of the 1950s and early 1960s that could represent the glory that was postwar America. In the 1960s, music began to explore social issues. The 1970s can be expressed in the more self-indulgent music such as disco. In the late 1970s and 1980s punk, metal, and grunge explored more sobering issues once again. And in the 1990s hip-hop and alternative music continued to push the boundaries and explore harder issues as well as entertain. Pop culture and music not only reflect the times, but as is evidenced from the social history of the late twentieth century, but can also be active social forces.

Economics alsoaffects pop culture and music. The postwar prosperity enabled music to flourish as a dynamic force. Record, cassette, and now CD sales reached new heights with every passing year. An essential component of media culture is knowledge and awareness of music fads and trends. The economic climate of the times is often reflected in the music (sound and lyrics) that is media. Economic and social issues are particularly evident in the music of the late 1960s, early 1970s, early and late 1980s, and much of the 1990s. Economics within music can be investigated as an exciting social efficacy theme in the teaching and learning process.

Technology has also provided impetus for the development of music as media culture and societal force. Incredible developments in the latter half of the twentieth century brought music to the masses, as well as enabling innovative sounds and techniques to be introduced. Electric guitars, synthesizers, and computers have had a substantial impact of the evolution of music. Television, MTV, CDs, and the Internet can all be investigated regarding their influence on music, media culture, and society. Technology has become a vital theme in society. Using technology as an agent in media culture can facilitate the idea of social efficacy, since technology and technology issues are so prevalent in today's society.

A controversial issue related to the growth of music as media culture is that of the influence of the music industry and the idea of corporate profits as the driving force for music. Central to the idea of media culture is issue of business and media music in the late twentieth century, through today is nothing if not business driven. And this is the constant struggle. Artists often provide empowering social efficacy messages but are also subject to personal sales. This often contradictory issue can provide much fodder for debate in the teaching and learning process. Issues related to capitalism, globalization, music choices, hegemony as the driving force, marketing, and how each relates to social efficacy could easily be integrated in schooling as we attempt to facilitate critical and active participation in society.

PROTEST MUSIC

Most music genres and many individual artists include songs that contain social commentary or historical references. Many people are under the assumption that social commentary in music reached its peak in the late 1960s and early 1970s. Punk, hip-hop, grunge, and alternative are genres from the 1980s through today that provide considerable social commentary and historical references. And even more traditional rock still has much to say regarding social efficacy and activism. And these are often the genres that most interest youth. While we may "just not understand" the music of today, we cannot become our parents and blindly dismiss its potential for critical social efficacy and activism. Remember the early folk and rock days.

Many forms of pop culture emerge as commentary or resistance toward more mainstream culture and society. Perhaps no better example of this exists than in pop music. From its earliest days pop has been viewed as cutting edge, crossing the boundaries, and a threat to the values and morals of society. Little Richard, Elvis Presley, the Beatles, Bob Dylan, the Rolling Stones, acid, heavy metal, disco, punk, MTV, grunge and thrash, rave, and hip-hop have all hadtheir detractors and have been viewed at one time or another as threats to the basic social fabric.

Through its history, pop culture has not only reflected the times but served as a catalyst for critical social efficacy and societal change. Music can be a powerful theme as we investigate issues such as ethnicity and the struggle for equality, population growth, economics, technology, business and industry, efficacy, and empowerment within the context of social history (Szatmary 2000).

Music in the United States, in the last part of the twentieth century at least, is often reflected through the struggle for equality by various ethnic groups, particularly African Americans. African American culture has played a crucial role in popular music, which would not exist without the blues, which originated from slave songs. Protest music of the 1960s often had civil rights as the predominant theme. African American artists are often the trailblazers in social commentary and music innovation including blues, jazz, R&B, disco, rap, and hip-hop. Each of these genres emerged as a proactive force with music doing more than perhaps any other societal force in promoting integration and appreciation of cultures.

Perhaps one of the most relevant issues surrounding music is its role as societal force, which relates directly to the issue of social efficacy and activism. Regardless of the genre, media music remains a vibrant cultural phenomenon that reflects societal issues but can also have a proactive impact. Exploring the role of music in reflecting and impacting societal change can be a motivating experience in the endeavor to make sense of the world. The idea that music, as well as supplying entertainment, can provide social commentary and perhaps even a call to arms for change makes it a powerful tool for social efficacy and activism.

The impact that music plays on the popular culture of people whom identified with its elements is hard to ignore but is readily dismissed by those who would claim that popular culture has no real significance to a population's development. Craig Watkins, professor of sociology, African American studies, and radio, television, and films knows exactly how cultural identity is maintained through the success of hip-hop and its impact on black youth (Roach 2004). Today's youth must struggle with issues like the deterioration of family, drug abuse, and violence, especially toward women. Even the band Everclear targets the emotional needs of many when the lyrics of "Father of Mine" detail the struggle of a family abandoned by the father. Other issues within the same ballad speak of spousal abuse and the problems faced when two cultures collide. These are significant issues in many students' worlds.

Why does censure seem so appealing? Again, music is often historically associated with rebellion and held responsible for many political events over the years. Most believe the 1950s to be the first turbulent time for music when efforts succeeded to a limited degree to censor Elvis Presley and his gyrating hips. However, censure attempts long preceded Elvis as the majority population tried to prevent music of ethnic origin to participate in mainstream America. Actually television may be held responsible for the increase in diversity of the music medium, because its creation would actually open doors for a greater variety of music, including African Americans, as radio air time became readily available and new artists could finally rally for their place in the world of music. The 1960s brought on the struggle for civil rights and as a result a new music genre ensued. For the first time in American history, racial lines were blurred when whites participated in a sound that developed in the African American culture. David P. Szatmary (2000) believes that music played an enormous role in the eventual integration of whites and blacks.

Although youth embraced this genre, parents revolted. In addition to social/racial considerations, the lines were drawn when many of the radical cultural and social changes that took place throughout the Western world in the 1960s were both reflected in and driven by music. Musicians like Phil Ochs and Country Joe and the Fish would openly rebel against the war in Vietnam and encourage a youthful society to join in this philosophy. Other popular artists would also reject the passivism of youth. Bob Dylan once remarked that "there's other things in this world besides love and sex that're important" (Szatmary 2000). He would encourage an entire generation to reject racism and other social evils to make a difference regardless of youthful appearance. This philosophy would not be embraced by the dominating culture, nor would it be the last time that this body would try to disparage popular artists. Marilyn Manson is a prime target of today's popular cultural icons. His image may seem despicable, but his message reveals a keen understanding of contemporary politics, not often evident in typical student psyches, so of course his views are widely criticized. While his messages may not reflect popular culture to most, they are reflections of at least one major part of society proven by the fact that his music sells.

Fewer artists are willing to maneuver their way into social controversy. The late Kurt Cobain (Ali 2002) once claimed that he blamed his parent's generation for

coming so close to social change then giving up after a few successful efforts by the media and government to deface the movement by using Mansons and other Hippie representatives as propaganda examples on how they were nothing but unpatriotic, communist, satanic, inhuman diseases.

Green Day defies this position with an album called *American Idiot*, which criticizes President Bush and the Iraqi War. The music obviously appeals to a wide audience as the album debuted at number 1 in September and has barely been out of the Top 10 since. Some would argue that popular artists like this have a duty to the public. Arundhati Roy (2001) determines that

> a great writer may refuse to accept any responsibility or morality that society wishes to impose on her. Yet the best and greatest of them know that if they abuse this hard-won freedom, it can only lead to bad art.

Roy realizes the duty to the public and the importance of separating "the strong, true, bright bird of the imagination from the synthetic, noisy bauble." What is important to remember is that what one culture deems bright and imaginative is a cacophony of incoherence to another. Whose role is it to determine where to draw the line? For Green Day, cutting through the incoherence was the motivation behind their successful album which earned a Grammy Award for best album in 2005. The message behind *American Idiot* defies youth's passive acceptance of media and challenges them to think for themselves.

While many may not agree with the message in the music as presented by popular music icons, these messages are indeed embraced by others. There is undeniable success associated with initiating critical conversations induced by bringing popular culture through music since so much of the messages explored by contemporary artists are reflections of the larger society.

Critics continue their argument regarding music's social effects on more than one level. Rosenthal (1998), reporting on his experience of teaching music and social movements at Wesleyan University, questions the actual function of music and whether or not it actually helps any movement. He claims that movements do not need music to be successful and conversely, music needs no movement to be popular. Other critics argue that the messages in today's music actually create the problems in our society and should not be given credence. This may be illustrated in two ways. First, this problem is most significant to researchers interested in the hip-hop generation, which often has included misogyny toward black females (Roach 2004). Second, sensitive political issues are prime discussion targets when artists like Rickie Lee Jones introduce songs like "Tell Somebody."

The strength of these issues defy Cobain's claim that the messages too often soothe the dominant culture, which is uncomfortable with images that reflect contemporary societal problems.

Activist artists like Eminem (Marshall Mathers III) have no problem revealing ugliness because the pain or rage within appeals to others through his sophisticated lyrics. Eminem's "Mosh," which was released shortly before the 2004 presidential election, provided a powerful message to fans of all ages. Using both animated and live footage, Eminem explores a variety of tough issues including the war in Iraq, racial profiling, and poverty. It seems that he intends to encourage youth to organize in a move for change. While he clearly blames the current political regime for the nation's ills, his lyrics offer solace through action.

He is a reflection of a growing culture that dominating forces would like to ignore or even silence. It comes as no surprise that the song garnered negative comments from the White House.

There are many others: Rise Against, System of a Down, Anti Flag, A Perfect Circle, Michael Franti, Ani Defranco, and Steve Earle among them. Much of the protest is centered around post 9-11 and the U. S. role in the world as played out by the Bush administration. Other related themes include critique of media such as Clear Channel (one of the reasons protest music is marginalized), issues with freedom and social justice in the U.S. the continued rise of the right in this country.

CONCLUSION

Music is a natural intrinsically motivating factor in our lives and should be celebrated for its potential in promoting social efficacy and activism. We are all very passionate about our likes and dislikes when it comes to popular music. Allowing for the investigation of issues regarding popular music as popular culture as Shukar suggests (1994) or using music as social and historical references as Szatmary (2000) suggests can only enhance critically active citizens. Again, a vital issue surrounding music is its role as societal force; as this relates most directly to the issue of social efficacy and activism. Yes, we have issues such as the Patriot Act, Clear Channel, and globalization affecting popular music. Nevertheless, popular music remains a vibrant cultural force that reflects societal issues but can also have a proactive impact. What better way to promote change or question authority than through music and its subsequent action?

REFERENCES

Ali, L. (2002). Cries from the heart. *Newsweek*, October 28, 60–68. Journals by Kurt Cobain published in 2002.

Garofalo, R., ed. (1992). *Popin' the boat: Mass music and mass movements.* Boston: South End Press. 1992.

Giroux, H. (1994). *Disturbing pleasures.* New York: Routledge.

Negus, K. *Producing pop: Culture and conflict in the media music industry.* London: Edward Arnold. 1992.

Roach, R. (2004). Decoding hip-hop's cultural impact. *Black Issues in Higher Education* 21(5): 30–32.

Rosenthal, R. (1998). Teaching a course on music and social movements. *Radical Teacher* 52: 15–20.

Roy, A. 2001. *Power politics.* Cambridge: South End.

Shuker, R. (1994). *Understanding media music.* New York: Routledge.

———. (1998). *Key concepts in media music.* New York: Routledge.

Szatmary, D. (2000). *Popin' in time: A social history of pop and roll.* Toronto: Prentice Hall.

Wallis, R., and Malm, K. (1992). *Media policy and music activity.* New York: Routledge.

White, C. (1999). *Transforming social studies: A critical perspective.* Springfield, IL: Thomas.

WEBSITES RELATED TO MUSIC AND PROTEST

Antiwar Songs: http://onegoodmove.org/1gm/1gmarchive/000628.html
Progressive Song Archive: www.zmag.org/songarchive.htm
Themed Songs: www.lacarte.org/songs/index.html
Activist Songs: www.ocap.ca/lyrics.html
Popular Songs in American History: www.contemplator.com/america
100 years of Music Posters: www.music-posters-history.com
This Day in Music History: http://datadragon.com/day
Black History in Music: www.rhino.com/blackhistory
Top 20 Music History: www.top20musichistory.com
Education Planet—History and Music: www.educationplanet.com/search/search?keywords=history+and+music&startval2=0
Songs for Social Studies: http://songsforteaching.homestead.com/SocialStudies.html
Teaching Media: www.media-awareness.ca/eng/med/class/teamedia/popcul.htm
Popular Culture Appreciation Society: http://home.vicnet.net.au/~popcult/net.htm#TOP

5

Historical Thinking

Learning to Read the Movies of History

Many states now describe their history curriculum as encompassing both knowledge and skills. Requirements may differ in the details, but the skill of critical thinking is common to many state standards. In Pennsylvania, for example, the definition of the subject reflects this importance: history is a "discipline that interprets and analyzes the past." This definition suggests that history teaching and learning should emphasize activities that give students opportunities to develop those critical thinking skills necessary to interpret and to analyze the people, places, and events of history.

There is a good deal of evidence that supports teaching critical thinking and problem solving skills to students at all levels, regardless of their ability, because all are capable to some degree. Although critical thinking has always been recognized as an important component in achieving the goal of citizenship education, it has never been a curricular or instructional priority in the schools. Rosenblum-Cale (1987) expressed this contradiction: "Thinking is a very natural act. What is unnatural is its scarcity" (p. 45). The emphasis in history classrooms on coverage of subject matter and recall of basic knowledge and understandings is problematic if students are to be prepared to reflect and work toward dealing with the pressing issues of our society. Students should be trained to think critically and have opportunities to practice these skills; good thinking and good citizenship are highly correlated.

Too often, unfortunately, history is text-driven and centers on the coverage/transmission of basic facts. Instruction in schools is primarily the transmission of information rather than the process of allowing students opportunities to interact with information and construct knowledge (Shor and Freire 1987). As teaching and learning objectives, transmission and recitation are used at the expense of developing problem solving and critical thinking skills. The teacher who is generally conditioned, due to reasons that are either intrinsic or extrinsic in nature, to go from one topic to another forgets to stop and take a critical look at the potential problem solving cases obvious throughout the history curriculum. Students grow comfortable being "taught to" so that they never ask the crucial questions of why or how. Most students learn to memorize facts, but few learn, or have the opportunity to learn, to think critically about those facts. If students are asked to think critically about history, then just by the sheer act of thinking critically, they take their learning a step further. They have engraved it deeper into their memory and then have the ability, as well as the habit of mind, to ask and understand how and why.

Offering students the opportunity to develop critical thinking skills does not diminish the importance of a knowledge base. Building critical thinking skills cannot effectively be done in general or in theory; students must know what they are to think about. An example I often use in my methods class is to ask students if Jack (from the beanstalk story) should be considered a hero or a villain. To discuss this, students must have knowledge of who Jack is, as well as an understanding of traits generally associated with heroes and villains. The important thing for teachers to remember is to not stop at that basic knowledge level.

There are many sources that may be used to provide students' an effective knowledge base in history. The most obvious and often used in the classroom are textbooks and the Internet. A less obvious resource is film. Gore Vidal (1986), through his fictional character *Myra Breckenridge*, observed that we have entered the post-Gutenberg period, a time when television and movies are more important than books. As a result, Vidal believes, the existing educational system should be scrapped and we should use movies to introduce students to the past. Carnes (1995) writes that this idea is "not that farfetched, nor even farsighted. Many history teachers of TV-besotted students have committed a fair proportion of instructional time to films" (p. 9).

Films are important cultural artifacts. As Mintz and Roberts (1993) point out, "Movies open windows into American cultural and social history . . . they provide a host of insights into Americans' shifting ideals, fantasies, and preoccupations" (pp. 1–2). Films can provide important truths about the human condition. This is especially true for films with popular appeal.

Popular movies, because of their commercial audience appeal, often reflect the ideas and attitudes of the era that produced them. Some films that were not originally regarded as historical have since become important historical documents. In fact, films that were originally considered historical often make more important statements about the era that produced them than the era they are trying to represent (Carnes 1995; Mintz and Roberts

1993). Carnes (1995) cites the following examples: *"Tea and Sympathy* explored tensions over homosexuality in the 1950s, and *Dr. Strangelove,* fears of nuclear deterrence in the 1960s . . . Cecil B. DeMille's lavish depiction of ancient Egypt in his *Ten Commandments* (1956), for example, served as a dusty mirror to the soulless materialism he perceived in 1950s America. Similarly, *Bonnie and Clyde* (1967) revealed more about gender in the Sixties than gangsters in the Thirties" (p. 10).

Films that overtly claim to portray something or someone from history can be useful to that end, but there is much greater potential in using films that might be realized. Often the main reason for using films that I hear from history teachers is to communicate some fact about history. Therefore the main activity asked of students, in addition to requiring them to watch the movie, has been either to recite events depicted (all involved assuming them to be historically accurate) or to question the historical accuracy of those depictions. I observed one high school history teacher who had shown her students the film *Glory* (1989) and then asked them questions such as, what was the number of buttons on the uniform of the Union soldier, and was that number correct (based on an earlier lecture she had given to them). Again, students must be provided opportunity to develop a knowledge base prior to being asked to think critically about it. However, films have much to offer beyond lower level cognitive activities.

Teachers who use films merely to communicate some historical information or facts accomplish no more than teachers who rely solely on textbooks and lecture. Teachers must expect more than passive receptivity from their students. This should be true of every educational endeavor, including the use of films in the classroom. More active and meaningful learning will result when students are asked to think, construct, and/or solve rather than memorize. Teachers should use films to develop students' critical thinking and problem solving skills. Students should be offered the opportunity to develop ideas rather than memorize facts. With most popular movies, higher level thinking skills may be employed to discover less overt ideas. Critical thinking and problem solving skills are not inherent in students and must be taught. Just as we teach young children to make meaning from the words in a written text, we can (and should) teach children to view for meaning. When the class sees its first movie, students must understand that the experience is equivalent to reading a book and will be treated the same way in the course of study.

In a history classroom, documentaries and historical movies are typically treated as statements of fact. Students are generally not required to think beyond the scenes presented. Popular movies on the other hand require critical thinking to make important connections to the periods in which they were made. Movies should be used to offer students opportunities to develop ideas rather than memorize facts. Viewing popular movies enables children to gather information directly and to gain knowledge through vicarious experiences. By watching these movies, children can develop empathy for others as well as a better understanding of their own feelings and values.

Movies to be used in the classroom should represent ideas, places, and/or characters that children will be able to relate to. Teachers need to begin with what the students already know, from life or some previous learning event. When children can relate their daily life experiences as well as prior knowledge to something they are watching, they are better able to understand and assimilate new concepts and knowledge (Alvermann, Smith, and Readance, 1985). Therefore, the engaging style of a popular movie may result in a student's understanding of a historical period (especially the one in which the movie was produced). Often, popular movies are packed with conceptual knowledge about the human condition and can supply meaningful content for skill-building experiences. A creative teacher can use popular movies to engage students in the pursuit of citizenship competencies as processing, examining other points of view, separating fact from opinion, and solving problems more completely, and certainly more intensely, than with textbooks.

THEORY TO PRACTICE:
TEACHING THE HISTORY OF PITTSBURGH

The above recommendations for effectively using films in the classroom can be incorporated into teaching and learning Pittsburgh's history. There are several commercial films to choose from that show places and/or people Pittsburgh school children know and can relate to. Constructing a lesson that builds on something that students have some prior knowledge of from life experience or previous learning event is a key factor in using movies to develop students' critical thinking and problem solving skills.

Four popular films, not meant to be historical when they were made, might be used in a classroom to allow students to construct a history of Pittsburgh from the postwar period to the present. Due to the popularity of the films, teachers might assume that filmmakers and audiences alike during the times these films were made found value and accuracy through the film portrayals. This makes them effective artifacts for investigation.

Prior to viewing the films and beginning to construct their history, students must have sufficient background content knowledge of each of these decades. This must exist before students can begin to think critically about the decade. Therefore this example might work best as a culminating project that emphasizes skill development. Even so, a review of significant people, places, and events of the decade should precede the showing of a film. The emphasis of the review should be on that content that would ultimately help students address the guiding question and analyze the film's historical period.

Films produced during each postwar decade (1950 to the 1990s) will give students another text and context in which to further examine the people, places, and events of the period. There are many people, places, and events that might be emphasized with students to give them an idea of a particular era. Just as there are also many films that could be chosen. The guiding questions that are included here are meant to provide an intentionally narrowed idea of the historical era. Ultimately, they are aimed at giving students the information necessary to develop the original assignment, constructing a people's history of Pittsburgh.

1950s
Main point for review:[1]
The Cold War
At the end of WWII, Americans became increasingly afraid of communism as embodied in the U.S.S.R. Many believed that it threatened the American way of life.

Guiding question:
As a citizen of Pittsburgh in the 1950s, what message about the American dream did *Angels in the Outfield* (1951) portray both to your fellow citizens and to the world, especially those that might be living in the Communist world.

Abbreviated plot summary (from the Internet Movie Database (IMDB)):
Angels in the Outfield (1951), NR (not rated)
A young woman reporter blames the Pittsburgh Pirates' losing streak on the obscenely abusive manager. While she attempts to learn more about him for her column, he begins hearing the voice of an angel promising him help for the team if he will mend his ways. As he does so, an orphan girl who is a Pirates fan and has been praying for the team begins noticing angels on the ballfield. Sure enough, the Pirates start winning, and McGovern tries to turn his life around. But can he keep his temper long enough for the Pirates to win the NL pennant?

Possible historical understandings regarding communist scare in the 1950s based on the film:
1. visual representation of "consensus" history (events for the community good) in 1950s America
2. the presence of angels: reconciling science and religion; communism was anti-religious
3. baseball as the great American past-time

[1]Main points were drawn from a high school history textbook: *The Americans: Reconstruction to the 21st Century*. 2003. Evanston Il: McDougal Littell

Figure 5.1. Lesson Plan) (*continues*)

1960s
Main point for review:
Civil Rights.
In 1960, segregation literally and figuratively divided the citizens of not just Pittsburgh, but of the entire United States. African Americans were denied access to jobs and housing, and were refused service at restaurants and stores. But the voices of the oppressed joined with those who supported rights for all citizens and together they took to the streets, demanding civil rights for all Americans.

Guiding question:
It's 1968 and you have just seen another nightly national news broadcast that touted the achievements in the work toward civil rights. But it seems that the tactics of some of those working toward the guarantee of civil rights for everyone had changed from the early '60s. Later that night you go to the movie theater to see *Night of the Living Dead* (1968) and suddenly begin to understand why the protestors had started becoming more confrontational. What makes you finally get it?

Abbreviated plot summary (from the Internet Movie Database (IMDB)):
Night of the Living Dead (1968) - NR (not rated)
Chaos descends upon the world as the brains of the recently deceased become inexplicably reanimated, causing the dead to rise and feed on human flesh. As the catastrophe unfolds, a young woman visiting her father's grave takes refuge in a nearby farmhouse, where she is met by an African American man who protects her and barricades them inside. They both later discover people hiding in the basement, and they each attempt to cope with the situation. Their only hope rests on getting some gasoline from a nearby pump into a truck that is running on empty, but this requires braving the hordes of ravenous walking corpses outside. When they finally put their plans into action, panic and personal tensions only add to the terror as they try to survive.

Possible historical understandings regarding race relations in the 1960s based on the film:
1) visual representation of "conflict" history (events call community into question) in 1960s America
2) visual representation of race relations in U.S./Pittsburgh; African American protagonist/hero who survives the zombie attacks only to be shot by a member of the local militia (that, not coincidentally, were all white)
3) images of police dog attacks on zombies are reminiscent of those in the American South

1970s
Main point(s) for review:
In the 1970s, many institutions, including the American workplace remained segregated environments.

Guiding question:
It is 1978, over a decade since Congress ruled that equality of opportunity must exist in voting and employment, and over two decades have passed since the Supreme Court ruled that separate was not equal. What do you learn about the American industrial workplace as well as "blue-collar" attitudes from watching the *Deer Hunter* (1978)?

Figure 5.1. (*continued*)

<u>Abbreviated plot summary (from the Internet Movie Database (IMDB)):</u>
Deer Hunter (1978), R^2

The first act of the film provides us with an inside look into the lives of a group of men from a small community who work and hang out together. Michael (Robert DeNiro) is shown early on as the natural leader of the group. After a days work, the men leave their jobs at a steel mill to head down to the local bar, where John (George Dzundza) works. Three of the men, Michael, Steven (John Savage), and Nick (Christopher Walken) will be leaving shortly for Vietnam, but not before Steven gets married. After the marriage, the group, including Axel (Chuck Aspegren) spends one last day on a hunting trip, one of their favorite past-times. This sequence of events enables us to view the lifestyle of a normal group of men, who will be suddenly and permanently affected by the ravages and separations of war.

<u>Possible historical understandings regarding equality and work life in the 1970s based on the film:</u>
  1) visual representation of the segregated nature of the industrial workplace even into 1970s America
  2) visual representation of the life of blue-collar workers in U.S./Pittsburgh
  3) inequities between those who served in Vietnam and those who did not

1980s
<u>Main point for review:</u>
In the 1980s, people in the United States began to experience economic hardships caused by the changing nature of the American economy. Industrial production became less profitable in the U.S. while at the same time becoming more profitable in countries like Japan. This resulted in a large number of workers losing their jobs, particularly in the automotive sector. Areas of the country that had once thrived in the more booming economies of heavy industry became known as "rust belts."

<u>Guiding question:</u>
Both your father and grandfather worked at the steel mill. You have always counted on working there too. But times have changed. The steel mill is downsizing and now laying off more workers than it is hiring. The entire local economy is depressed. What do you learn about this new corporate economy and its winners and losers from the movie *Gung Ho* (1986)?

<u>Abbreviated plot summary (from the Internet Movie Database (IMDB)):</u>
Gung Ho (1986) – *PG13*

In the 80's American, and Japanese auto makers were bitter rivals. Company cultures were different, and Americans everywhere feared an invasion of Japanese products into even more facets of the American economy. It appeared to everyone that while the U.S. economy was in decline, the Japanese economy was growing stronger. In the 80's movie *Gung Ho* these tensions are presented in a most unique fashion. An American auto-plant is purchased and retooled to manufacture cars for a Japanese company. This transaction

---

[2]If teachers have concerns about showing films that are rated *R* to their students, these might be eliminated by showing clips from the movie rather than the entire film.

Figure 5.1. (*continues*)

saves countless jobs for a small town. Michael Keaton plays an American Auto worker that attempts to bridge the gap between American workers and Japanese managers which have just arrived to run the plant. Despite cultural differences, the Japanese are determined to see this new American plant produce as efficiently as plants back home in Japan.

<u>Possible historical understandings regarding the new economy of the 1980s based on the film</u>:
1) American workers suffered hardships and uncertainty as the economy began to transform from an industrial base to a technological one
2) the interests of business are sometimes privileged over individuals and society
3) culture of the Japanese workplace differed greatly from the American workplace; many U.S. industries adopted elements of the Japanese system to gain a competitive edge

1990s
<u>Main point for review</u>:
In the 1990s the economic hardships of the 1980s, which also brought about crime increases, lessened. Pittsburgh began to reinvent itself as a technology center rather than an industrial one.

<u>Guiding question</u>:
Pittsburgh's long history as an industrial city gives it a reputation of being dirty and gritty – both ecologically and otherwise. However, the movie *Inspector Gadget* (1999) lets you see another view of Pittsburgh. What does the new Pittsburgh look like?

<u>Abbreviated plot summary (from the Internet Movie Database (IMDB))</u>:
Inspector Gadget (1999) - PG
Matthew Broderick plays the security guard who is physically transformed into a multi-use cyborg with a zillion attachments, from stilts to helicopter blades to skis. A crime-fighter in raincoat and fedora, and equipped with a nifty *Gadgetmobile*, the hero investigates the death of a man linked to the villainous Sanford Scolex (Rupert Everett) also known as the *Claw*. Scolex, or the Claw, who blames Gadget for having to wear a prosthetic hand, develops an evil robot twin of the good inspector, causing much mischief.

<u>Possible historical understandings regarding the technologically based reinvention of Pittsburgh in the 1990s based on the film</u>:
1) new technologies are not always for the better
2) new technologies require oversight and regulation
3) just because you can do something, doesn't mean that you should
Figure 5.1. (*continued*)

CONCLUSION

In a history classroom, documentaries and historical films are typically treated as statements of facts. Students are generally not required to think beyond the scenes presented. Popular films are cultural artifacts and as such require critical historical thinking to make important connections to the periods in which they were made. The use of film as a primary source will provide students opportunities to develop their own ideas rather than memorize facts.

With most popular films, higher-level thinking skills may be employed to discover less overt ideas. Critical thinking and problem solving skills are not inherent in students and must be taught. Just as we teach young children to make meaning from the words in a written text, we can (and should) teach children to view for meaning. When the class sees its first movie, students must understand that the experience is equivalent to reading a book and will be treated the same way in the course of study.

More active and meaningful learning will result when students are asked to think, construct, and/or solve rather than memorize. Teachers who use films merely to communicate historical information or facts, however well intentioned they may be, accomplish no more than teachers who rely solely on textbooks and lecture. Films read as literal text often generate the same level of passive receptivity among students as printed textbooks do. History teachers must set higher-level expectations for their students. This should be true of every educational endeavor, including the use of films in the classroom.

REFERENCES

Alvermann, D., Smith, I., Readance, J. (1985). Prior knowledge activation and the comprehension of compatible and incompatible text. *Reading Research Quarterly* 20: 244–67.

Brown, C. (1951). *Angels in the Outfield*. Dir. C. Brown. Metro-Goldwyn-Mayer.

Carnes, M. (1995). *Past imperfect: History according to the movies*. New York: Holt.

Deer Hunter. (1978). Dir. M. Cimino. Universal Pictures.

Glory. (1989). Dir. E. Zwick. Tri-Star Pictures

Gung Ho. (1986). Dir. R. Howard. Paramount Pictures.

Inspector Gadget. (1999). Dir. D. Kellogg. Walt Disney Pictures.

Mintz, S., and Roberts, R. (1993). *Hollywood's America: United States history through its films*. St. James, NY: Brandywine.

Night of the Living Dead. (1968). Dir. G. Romero. Image Ten.

Rosenblum-Cale, K. (1987). *Teaching thinking skills: Social studies*. Washington, DC: National Education Association.

Shor, I., and Freire, P. (1987). *A pedagogy for liberation: Dialogues on transforming education*. Westport, CT: Bergin & Garvey.

Vidal, G. (1986). *Myra Breckinridge*. New York: Random House.

6

Moral Panic

Schools and the Battle for Anime

Every generation has its pop culture icons. Some think back fondly on hula-hoops, clackers, pet rocks, and mood rings. In the last decade we have seen pogs, Ninja Turtles, virtual pets, and Beanie Babies. The anime craze has now lasted for several years. Kids of all ages are playing anime video games and collecting and trading anime cards. One finds anime on television sometimes twice a day, a new anime movie, collectors' books, trade and comic books, and toys of all kinds. It has become a pop culture phenomenon and industry. The difference is that anime offers a real opportunity for educators. If we listen closely to our children, we will find that anime cards promote critical thinking, problem solving, reading skills, math skills, and conflict resolution. One needs only listen to kids in the hallways of their schools, on the playgrounds, at lunch, on buses to and from home, and on the soccer field to find children that are truly excited and engaged with anime.

We find it easy to criticize anime, and this may very well be the issue. It is all about competition, commercialism, and fighting. Adults dismiss these components as harmful to our kids. Yet our kids are much smarter than we give them credit for. They realize early on that their world (and, yes, the adult world too) is dominated by competition, commercialism, and fighting. Why not use these in an issues-centered or problem-based approach in teaching and learning?

The anime card game is every bit as complex and high-level as games like Risk, general war games, or other games of strategy. The difference is that it has become an essential part of our popular culture. Kids of all ages are collecting cards and participating in various anime activities, and they are bringing their parents (perhaps screaming) into the culture.

An entire anime subculture has arisen. And who are we to dismiss this trend as a negative influence in our children's lives? Creating a world of caring and compassion requires the cultivation of the human spirit, the nourishment of the imagination, and the impulse for self-expression (Purpel and Shapiro 1995).

THE POP CULTURE DEBATE

Popular culture is always at the center of societal debate, particularly as it applies to children. Regardless of this debate, we need to understand that popular culture is part of our lives and is very important to our society, our citizens, and especially our children. Nevertheless, integrating popular culture in teaching and learning and to facilitate critical inquiry has great possibility for education. If this be so, we need to better integrate popular culture in the education process, and anime is a powerful possibility.

We owe it to our kids to provide opportunities for critical analysis of popular culture. Rather than ignoring or censoring popular culture such as anime, we can use it as teachable opportunities. The idea is to meaningfully integrate popular culture as an alternative text. This is vital if we are to employ popular culture and childhood desire to promote knowledge, skills, and values exploration among our children.

INTEGRATING POPULAR CULTURE

Film, television, music, and other forms of popular culture can provide rich opportunities for teaching and learning in our schools. Unfortunately, children experience few opportunities to engage popular culture except outside of school. Even in the workplace, conversation often revolves around popular culture events. Why then do we avoid popular culture in the classroom? Our children's natural desire to make sense of their world can be enhanced through the appreciation and application of "their pop culture icons" such as anime as teaching and learning tools. Popular culture can provide the common connections and voice for our often disconnected youth that many of us remember as wide-eyed joy and sense of wonder of the world (White 2003).

Popular culture can counter the trend toward scripting lessons and standardizing teaching. If we are truly interested in kids being motivated to learn, then we must make stronger efforts at integrating meaningful curriculum and instruction that includes real world connections. These connections allow kids to develop the scaffolding needed to construct knowledge. Popular culture can enhance a transformative rather than transmissive learning experience by providing these connections. If this be so, we need to better integrate popular culture in the education process. It is precisely in the diverse spaces and spheres of popular culture that most of the education that matters today is taking place on a global scale (Giroux 1994).

ANIME POSSIBILITIES

Educators now have a grand opportunity. Instead of dismissing the phenomenon and overreacting to its prevalence by banning and punishing, we could use Anime as a powerful teaching tool. When was the last time any teacher (or parent for that matter) saw kids glow with passion like they do when "talking Anime?" And Anime is really just the metaphor—many popular culture icons of the past could be used for facilitating knowledge, skills, and values-exploration.

Anime is enjoyed by kids of many ages, with kids from 5—up are playing various Anime themed video games. Little kids are developing their own playing rules, engaging in creative role/dramatic play, setting up Anime (Pokemon, Digemon) stands (the lemonade stand of the new millennium) in their front yards, and processing names, descriptions, and numbers at an amazing pace. As all kids negotiate and trade cards, they are demonstrating very high levels of reading, creativity through drawing and writing, and intrinsic motivation where this game is becoming not only their game of choice, but a device that promotes interactions. They do the same with the video games, creating alternate play experiences from creating their own games and characters to writing their own stories.

Unfortunately, many of our schools have reacted to Anime the way we typically react to things we do not understand. Teachers and administrators witnessed kids trading, gambling, selling, and discussing Anime cards. This "inappropriate and off-task" behavior is perceived as taking away from real learning. The traditional reactionary mindset has reared its ugly head yet again. Administrators and teachers are banning Anime and punishing kids who break the newly established rules. And video games are never mentioned in schools except as negative influences. Instead of over-reacting to this fad, we could use Anime as a very powerful teaching tool.

If we would only take time to look closely, we might see that Anime could enhance many of our educational guiding principles. What kind of knowledge and skills are promoted? What inquiry, values exploration, and processes are facilitated? The following represent some of the ways we can make Anime part of the students' educational experience (even in schools).

Meaningful teaching and learning. It is important to make the learning relevant and meaningful to the students' school and community. This means developing curriculum and instruction that children can relate to—A focus

Table 6.1. Concepts Emerging from Anime

Mathematics

Number sense	Hit points and needed energy, monster numbers, and card
Number and operations	numbers.
Patterns	Multiplying hit points, adding or subtracting resistance and
Probability	weaknesses.
Estimation	Energy patterns
Measurement	Coin flipping to reverse attacks. To determine attack
Place value	strategies and energy needed.
	Anime character data are described in length and weight.
	Damage counters (1 damage counter = 10 damage).

Science

Evolution	Evolution stages.
Growth and patterns	Creatures evolve or grow from other creatures (i.e.,
Defense mechanisms	Bulbasaur to Ivysaur; Weedle to Kakuna to Beedrill).
Basic elements and states	Attack text, flavor text (i.e., spits fire)
of matter	Energy cards and Anime types (i.e., fire, water, or
Predator/prey relationships	colorless).
	Attack strategies.

Social Studies

Economics	Card editions. Encouragement to trade to create stronger
Culture	decks and collect all the creatures.
Social skills development.	Rules for playing and trading.
Values exploration and	Cards and information in Japanese.
development.	Conflict resolution.

Literacy

Phonemic awareness and	Names of creatures such as Alakazam, Beedreill,
syllabication	Dragonair, Charmeleon, and Squirtle.
Oral communication	Kids talking, strategizing, trading, etc.
Reading	Card text, books, comics, instructions.
Myths and mythology	Terms such as metronome, agility, etc.
Storytelling	
Dramatic play	

on student-driven curriculum originating from what their know and are interested in is the first step. Examples include the school, classroom, neighborhood, family, and community and issues and events that arise from these areas such as Anime. Kids talk Anime from the time they get up until the time they go to bed. Their pockets and backpacks are full of cards and conversations with peers are engaging and strategic.

Challenging teaching and learning. It is important to empower decision-making through challenging higher level activities. Allow students to make decisions and live with the decisions they make by engaging in inquiry, cooperative learning, and simulations. Anyone who has read the rules for Anime understands that the number and complexity of possible moves requires students to have learned the game while working with others, asking many questions, and simulating possible attacks, retreats, and diversions.

Integrative teaching and learning. Integrate between disciplines, but also among the areas within traditional subject areas. Table 1 illustrates some of the content components that are explicit and prevalent as kids play the game. In addition to these it takes a variety of skills such as decision-making, problem-solving, and critical thinking to build decks, learn the game, and play the game.

Value-based teaching and learning. Allow for controversy and story by presenting all sides of the issue. Integrate strategies that encourage diverse viewpoints such as debates, role-playing, inquiry, and issue investigations. Talk about the game, its appropriate use and play. Examine the issues involved in inappropriate use like gambling or stealing.

Active teaching and learning. Traditional teaching and learning has been passive and teacher-directed. Active involvement of children is necessary for students. There is no question that Anime promotes active participation by students. Channeling that activity for learning is the challenge educators have with this popular culture game.

STUDENT VIEWS

We talked to 25 students from ages 6-10 in small groups about Anime. Here are some of their comments. Following are the questions we asked the kids.

"Why do you like Anime?"

"What kinds of things do you do with Anime?"

"What have you learned by doing things with Anime?"

"How could your teacher and school use Anime in the classroom?"

The first question didn't prompt many different answers, but the kids could have talked about Anime all day. The excitement was amazing. One 8-year old said it was the best fad he had ever seen. Others said:

"It's fun, cool; I like the characters."

"It comes from Japan and they have cool ideas for monsters."

"It's different, like colors, shapes, and characters."

"It's not like anything else."

"You can do all kinds of things with the cards."

The second question, "What kinds of things do you do with Anime?" elicited many responses from all ages. Young kids mostly collect the cards and watch the cartoon. They also play their own version of the game. All the kids knew all the characters, their hit points, and who should win over whom. All knew the basic premise of the cartoon. Sample responses include:

"I collect them and play the game."

"We pretend to be Anime or play with Anime with Beanie Babies or something else."

"It's fun to just talk about the cards and trade them."

"I watch the cartoon and play the video game."

"I make my own Anime characters and draw the real ones."

"It's kinda like war, only for play."

"I set up my own Anime room with posters, hiding places, cards, and a place to play Anime."

"I set up a Anime store in my yard. I sold 6."

The third question is, "What kinds of things have you learned with Anime?" It is interesting to see if kids recognize that they may truly be learning something from the game. During the interviews, their comments about playing the game were very telling about how much they are learning. One 9-year old said, "The game has been around for over a year and has made 5 billion dollars, that's nine zeros." Another 6 year old said, " I took 30 minus 20, that is 10, and then doubled it because it is 10 plus 10 here." In response to this question students said:

"I learned some math and how to spell all the names."

"How to make trades. I need three of the same cards to trade one. One to play, one to sell, and one to trade."

"These cards can be expensive. Like if it's a star, it's worth more money, diamonds are in the middle, and circles are worth only a little."

"Not much for your brain."

"I like to hear about Japan now."

"I learned some new words like evolution."

"I learned what a fair trade is and what isn't."

"I learned that if you're nice, people may trade you more."

The final question is "How could your teacher or school use Anime for teaching?" Responses to this question included:

"For math, you have to know how to add and subtract, maybe even multiply."

"For math, you need to know how many hit points and who has the most hit points."

"Learning codes and making guessing games."

"It's like taking care of pets, knowing what they need for energy."

"There's a trainer that recycles."

"You can make up new games, stories, and songs with them."

"They could use it for reading, new words like metronome, guillotine, and agility are hard words."

"How to spell."

"How to draw better."

"How not to waste your money, knowing when to trade, buy new packs, or just buy power packs."

CONCLUSION

Popular culture embodies a language of both critique and possibility; a language that allows students to locate themselves in history, find their own voices, and establish convictions and compassion necessary for democratic civic courage (Freire and Giroux 1989). The creators of Anime have done a wonderful marketing job. The first page of the instruction manual says, "Carry your Anime cards with you and you're ready for anything! You've got the power in your hands, so use it!" The same goes for popular video games. Those are important instructions to kids who are geared up and ready to collect them all, so we can either fight them or join them and use the game, while it lasts, as a teaching and learning tool. This is not the first or the last bit of popular culture that will come our way. It is important that we look at its strengths and weaknesses and how we can use it to our education advantage. "May the force be with you" and may your own pop culture dreams come true.

REFERENCES

Freire, P., and Giroux, H. (1989). Pedagogy, popular culture, and public life. In H. Giroux and R. Simon, eds., *Popular culture: Schooling and everyday life.* Granby, MA: Bergin & Garvey.

Giroux, H. (1994). *Disturbing pleasures.* New York: Routledge.

Purpel, D., and Shapiro, S. (1995). *Beyond liberation and excellence.* Westport, CT: Bergin & Garvey.

Steinberg, S., and Kincheloe, J. (1997). *Kinderculture: The corporate construction of childhood.* Boulder: Westview.

White, C. 1999. Popular culture and the teaching of social justice. *Encounter* 12(3): 33–38.

7

Global Toppings

What Pizza Tells Us about the World

When I growing up in a small town in southeast Texas during the 1960s and 1970s, pizza was the first foreign food I ever ate. Interestingly, we did not consider Mexican food foreign. Now when I think about how big the world seemed back then, and yet how small the piece I knew about was, it is a little sad. Although thinking about how we ever considered pizza a foreign food is a little funny. I wonder how many kids today, even those in my small town, would have such a limited exposure to the world—or still consider pizza a foreign food.

Today the world is a smaller place. Communication is instantaneous and actual travel to even the most remote parts of the world is possible and relatively rapid. Schools in the United States must provide opportunities for students to learn about the world: who the people are, what they do, and how they live. Students must learn how to get along with all people—in the United States and the world—as responsible citizens of both. Education for civic competence, for responsible national and world citizenship, falls within the domain of social studies instruction and learning.

A CASE FOR GLOBAL EDUCATION

Social studies must include education for a global perspective so that students may become competent, active citizens of the world (Tucker and Evans 1996; Diaz, Massialas, Xanthopoulos 1999; Chapin 2003). A critical component of education in general, and social studies specifically, is to promote an understanding of diversity at home and abroad, "integrating global realities within an existing social studies curriculum meets the needs of an ever-changing, ethnically diverse, increasingly interdependent, international community" (Tucker and Evans 1996, 189). World citizenship requires a global education.

Global education efforts must begin with an attempt to understand globalization. Globalization can be defined as "the intensification of worldwide social relations which link distant localities in such a way that local happenings are shaped by events occurring many miles away and vice versa" (McLaren 1995, 180). Diaz, Massialas, and Xanthopoulos (1999) state that globalization

> refers to the compression of the world and to the intensification of the consciousness of the world as a whole. This process is ongoing and all of us, young and old, Westerners and nonWesterners, are inescapably involved in it. The compression of the world is real. People witness it in their daily lives, in the foods they eat, in the TV programs they watch, in the cars they drive, in the dresses and costumes, in the people they choose to govern them, and so on. (pp. 37–38)

Clearly globalization is increasingly influential in all aspects of life. Therefore understanding it through global education is imperative. Schools must provide opportunities for children to "develop the appropriate cognitive skills to understand and explain the globalization process and to critically analyze its impact on their lives and the lives of people around them" (Diaz, Massialas, Xanthopoulos 1999, 38). Above all, according to Diaz, Massialas, and Xanthopoulos (1999), students need to know how to impact the global system as world citizens and as advocates of a well-grounded position or point of view. This suggests that students must acquire both a new knowledge base and a skill set. Many of the subjects associated with social studies might offer an appropriate space for global education. Given that at its core, global education is about cultures and people of other lands (Chapin 2003), a likely fit might be found in geography instruction.

RETHINKING GEOGRAPHY INSTRUCTION
IN THE UNITED STATES

Members of the Geography Education Standards Project published grade-level expectations to explain what students should know and be able to do in geography. Their publication, *Geography for life: National Geography Standards 1994*, went beyond school-based standards to encourage lifelong learning in geography. The National Geographic Society followed this first attempt at national standards with publications in 2000 and 2001 that outlined the scope and sequence of geography education. However, reports from NAEP and other studies continue to show that people of all ages in the United States, especially young people, are not very knowledgeable of geography. The evidence suggests that people have difficulty locating places on a map and have poor recall of the names of capital cities, but are these really the most important measures of geographic knowledge and skills? Kincheloe (2001) refers to this memorization of facts in conceptual isolation as the "flax mentality" (p. 676).

Teachers should fight the flax mentality by asking students to apply their knowledge in a meaningful context. Kincheloe (2001) provides the example of introducing high school students to metaphysical speculation via the fifth-century century geographical scholar, Herodotus. He explains that students gain interesting insights about the subjectivity of maps when they examine them in the contexts of the world view of the time and the cosmology of Herodotus (pp. 676–677).

Chapin (2003) also supports geography instruction that goes away from the flax mentality:

> Geography organizes both the human and physical information about the world so that people better understand its nature . . . uniting the physical and the cultural world in the study of people, places, and environments. Geography points out how "the local" affects "the global" and vice versa." (p. 165)

The study of geography in the United States could provide the opportunity to grow our understanding and appreciation of others in the world, something essential to our roles and responsibilities as global citizens. Given the global interconnectedness of the world today, the global context must be present. According to Merryfield (2001), students must develop a global perspective that will emphasize cross-cultural experiential learning and stress commonalities in cultures that transcend diversity. One culture that already seems to transcend world barriers is popular culture.

POPULAR CULTURE AND THE GLOBAL POPULAR

Common culture or mass culture is usually defined as "popular culture." Today, popular culture is more specifically associated with commercial culture: movies, television, radio, advertising, toys, photography, games, the Internet, and so on. Popular culture is also one of the most lucrative U.S. exports; some reports list popular culture exports second only to the aerospace industry in total revenue.

The export of popular culture is not a new phenomenon. Elements of popular culture have always spread beyond national borders. One of the earliest examples is from the eighth century B.C.E. as Homer's epic poems, *The Iliad* and *The Odyssey*, spread throughout the oral societies of the

Balkans. Today satellite television, multinational media corporations, and the Internet provide unprecedented opportunities for the spread of popular culture. U.S. students have access to media that allows them to experience cultures from around the world. Conversely, many of these culture "indus- tries" are U.S. exports, so world access to American popular culture is also burgeoning. Given the global cross-cultural nature of contemporary popu- lar culture, it is sometimes difficult to determine origin. This globalization of popular culture has resulted in what Kellner (1995) refers to as a new *global popular*.

The existence of the global popular means that we might easily find a common frame of reference or topic when asking U.S. students to consider others in the world. One such topic or frame is pizza. An investigation of pizza may be facilitated by the Internet and the availability of online sites from one of the largest pizza restaurant chains today—Pizza Hut.

READING PIZZA HUT IN GEOGRAPHY CLASS

Students today live in a world made up of many texts, and it is essential that they develop multiple literacies that will allow them to read the signs, sym- bols, and images (texts) of that world. Schools must provide students with "new operational and cultural 'knowledges' in order to acquire new lan- guages that provide access to new forms of work, civic and private practices in their everyday lives" (Lankshear and Knoble 2003, 11). Social studies classes seem to be the perfect place to turn students on to these meaningful knowledges/issues and popular culture can provide the context for devel- oping the literacy skills necessary to interpret those issues. Students must begin to think critically about popular culture texts. The word "text" is gen- erally anything that can take on meaning—events, places, images, sounds, gestures, and so forth. The literacy (decoding and comprehension) skills re- quired to make sense of these texts are complicated by the fact that these texts can take on different meanings depending on the situation, context, usage, culture, or historical period (Gee 2003). Students must critically ex- amine assumptions, attitudes, and values underlying the production, medi- ation, and consumption (especially students' own consumption) of such texts and how they position students to assume particular social, gendered, and racial reading positions (Ellsworth 1990) as they invite them to explore a constructed world in particular ways.

Reading global pizza texts as part of the geography curriculum offers stu- dents the opportunities to apply knowledge and develop skills in a mean- ingful context, as Kincheloe (2001) recommends. Students learn where people live, their environments, and so on. They also learn that what peo- ple eat is determined mainly by location, although occasionally also by religious beliefs (which some historians argue can also be tied in origin to location). These things are revealed through an examination of their popular culture, which is especially noticeable in what they eat on their pizza.

A quick Google search will confirm the universality of pizza and reveal the largest global pizza restaurant chain, Pizza Hut. While other types of food franchises may be as numerous, or even outnumber the Pizza Hut shops in the world, pizza, because of its takeout and delivery options, was the easiest to do this type of investigation. Pizza Hut restaurants around the world post their menus and prices online to facilitate ordering. Given the transient nature of the Internet—some sites here today and gone tomorrow—the investigation of global Pizza Huts required a website that would link together the various URLs, making sure that they were working, that English translations of the menus were available, and so on. A website that provided more context for their study by including a clickable world map through which the Pizza Hut URLs would be accessed would encourage an orderly investigation of countries around the world. I designed just such a website: www.vancouver.wsu.edu/fac/walkert/globalpizzahutlesson.html.

The opening page of the site explains:

> Pizza is universal. People around the world use and understand the word. But what is pizza? There seems to be no central definition of pizza: it's not always round, the crust isn't always made of dough, the sauce isn't always made from tomatoes. It turns out that pizza means different things to different people. We can learn many things about people and the places where they live based on what they put on their pizzas. Like what? Why don't you check out a few of the Pizza Hut menus from around the world and find out? You'll discover a few things about your global neighbors and their neighborhoods. And you might even learn something about yourself.

Currently on my website there are twenty-two live links to Pizza Huts around the world. One way to get started with students might be to have them go through a couple of the menus to look for pizza toppings that sound strange or interesting. There are a number of food items other than pizza that might also be considered. For instance, the Hong Kong menu includes a section called "Tea Set." The dishes under this category seem to be smaller and lighter fare than other main menu options—a bit like the meal that the British refer to as "tea." Also, one of the dishes, "Meaty Mashed Potato," looks similar to a British dish—Shepherd's Pie. If students consider the British influence on the Hong Kong Pizza Hut menu, both in name and dish substance, there are obvious connections between Hong Kong and Great Britain. Students can practice their inquiry and critical thinking skills to gain information that otherwise might have been found in a history book or atlas but in a less challenging way. There might also be students who wonder why a large pizza in Hong Kong costs over $100. What must annual income be if pizza costs this much? Or does the cost mean that pizza is a gourmet experience and therefore a special treat? Or does it mean that Hong Kong dollars are not valued the same as U.S. dollars and must be converted for the costs of pizza to make sense?

There are many other possible lines of inquiry with the Pizza Hut menus. One relatively powerful investigation might ask students to look at pizzas for hints about a country's predominant religious group. I have included two examples to demonstrate this inquiry. I included only pizza items here; however, there are numerous other items on the menus that could also have been used.

Example 1: Sri Lanka's *Develled Beef* Pizza
http://www.pizzahut.lk

A traditional atlas reflects the following information for Sri Lanka (formerly Ceylon). It is a small island in the Indian ocean of 25,332 square miles located just off the southeastern coast of India.[1] They use the same currency as in India, the rupee. Sri Lanka has a population of 19 million, a tropical climate, lush green forests, and a rich history.

It's proximity to India might indicate a predominately Hindu population. However, a quick glance at the pizza featured above would suggest that this is not true. In fact, Buddhism is the predominant religion in Sri Lanka. There are several different beef selections on the Pizza Hut menu in Sri Lanka which would not be the case if the population was predominately made up of non–beef eating Hindus as in India.

Example 2: Philippines *Spam Lovers* Pizza
http://www.pizzahut.com.ph/main.php?p=flash

The Philippines are a group of islands in Southeast Asia, located in the South China Sea, just east of Vietnam. Their total area is 115,830 square miles and population is 79,345,812. The climate is tropical and pineapples are the major crop. In fact, pineapple has a wide variety of uses there. Pineapple fiber is woven into clothing.

Malaysia and Indonesia are located near the Philippines. Both these countries are predominately Islamic and given its proximity, the Philippines might be also. Spam, the primary ingredient in the *Spam Lovers* pizza pictured above, is made from a combination of meats (best not considered to any great degree). One known meat in Spam is ham—pork. The preponderance of pork toppings, especially bacon, clearly reveals that the majority of the population is not Islamic. The majority of the population in the Philippines is Christian. In fact, it is the only Christian country in Asia. This is an obvious link to its history as a Spanish colony, not coincidentally Spain's only colony in Asia.

CONCLUSION

Responsible global citizenship requires knowledge of others in the world. It also requires the skills to understand and act in the best interest of the majority of the people. The knowledge base should include an understanding of who the other people in the world are, what they do, and where they are. The skill set should include inquiry and critical literacy/thinking skills. Geography instruction must avoid the flax mentality and provide students opportunities to apply their knowledge in a meaningful context. Popular culture is a global frame that contains various texts that can be used effectively in a classroom. One of those texts is pizza. The global appetite for pizza makes it a good choice for looking at the people and places in the world.

NOTE

1. All the "flax mentality" information was found in the 2001 *Scholastic Atlas of the World*.

REFERENCES

Barber, B. (2001). *Jihad vs. McWorld: Terrorism's challenge to democracy*. New York: Ballantine.

Chapin, J. (2003). *A practical guide to secondary social studies*. Boston: Pearson Education.

Diaz, C., Massialas, B., Xanthopoulos, J. (1999). *Global perspectives for educators*. Boston: Allyn & Bacon.

Gee, J. (2003). *What video games have to teach us about learning and literacy*. New York: Palgrave.

Geography Education Standards Project. (1994). *Geography for life: National geography standards, 1994*. Washington, DC: National Geographic Society.

Kellner, D. (1995). *Media culture: Cultural studies, identity, and politics between the modern and the postmodern*. London: Routledge.

Kincheloe, J. (2001). *Getting beyond the facts: Teaching social studies/social sciences in the twenty-first century*. New York: Lang.

Lankshear, C., and Knobel, M. (2003). *New literacies: Changing knowledge and classroom learning*. Buckingham, UK: Open University Press.

McLaren, P. (1995). *Critical pedagogy and predatory culture: Oppositional politics in a postmodern era*. New York: Routledge.

Merryfield, M. (2001). Moving the center of global education: From imperial world views that divide the world to double consciousness, contrapuntal pedagogy, hybridity, and cross-cultural competence. In W. Stanley, ed., *Critical issues in social studies research for the 21st century,* 179–207. Greenwich, CT: Information Age Publishing.

Tucker, J., and Evans, A. (1996). The challenge of a global age. In B. Massialas and R. Allen, eds., *Crucial issues in teaching social studies K-12,* 181–218. Belmont, CA: Wadsworth.

8

Kidstory

Social Education through Kid Culture and TV Cartoons

What is the role of kid (popular) culture in schools and society? Does kid (popular) culture have a role in the education process of our young? Kid culture plays a very prominent role in our lives and is very important to our society, our citizens, and especially our children. In a society increasingly fragmented by debate, misunderstandings, and lack of consensus, perhaps kid culture remains one of the few arenas that provide a forum for common understandings, dialog, and communication, at least for our kids. If this is so, we need to better integrate kid culture in the education process. It is precisely in the diverse spaces and spheres of kid culture that most of the education that matters today is taking place on a global scale (Giroux 1994).

Education should be aware and unafraid of childhood desire, often connecting it to children's efforts to understand the world and themselves (Steinberg and Kincheloe 1997). Childhood desire is a natural phenomenon that is unfortunately often driven and dictated by the dominant culture. The idea is to critically analyze these issues and also provide the critical efficacy children need so as to facilitate this natural desire and wonder for learning about and coping with their world. This is vital if we are to employ kid culture and childhood desire to promote social education.

A strong argument can be made that kid culture has become the most influential education institution for our children in society, and many seem frustrated by this (Buckingham 1998). Our society has made kid culture a cornerstone of cultural identity and we simply cannot ignore that fact. Television, movies, music and other media provide fodder for connections among our disconnected citizenry. Why not use this, rather than belittle it? We owe it to our kids to provide opportunities for critical analysis of kid culture. Rather than blindly accepting the "Disneyfication" or "Simpsonizing" of our kids and their lives, use them as teachable opportunities. Film, television, music, and other forms of kid culture can provide rich opportunities for teaching and learning (Steinberg and Kincheloe 1997).

TUNING IN

Kid culture such as movies, television, music, media, toys, technology, sports, food, fashion, and fads can be used in a number of ways in education. Integrating kid culture for social education can enhance a critical and active citizenry able to think for itself and engage in problem solving. The idea of providing voice and empowering kids with meaningful, challenging, integrative, value-based and controversial, and active teaching and learning should be the goal (NCSS 1994). And kid culture offers a natural integration. Just imagine the power of movies, television, music, media, toys, technology, and fads.

Our schools are still floundering in the "information as knowledge" mind-set that has dictated teaching and learning for so long. And with the upsurge in accountability and high-stakes testing to ensure "knowledge," this is more entrenched than ever. All stakeholders are caught in the middle of what many consider an overreaction to the state of schools and education as a cause for society's ills. Apple and Beane suggest issues including home schooling, charter schools, test preparation as essential curriculum, prison-like schools, and both kids and teachers bored and demeaned into submission (Apple and Beane 1995).

But what better way to enhance the idea of social education than to employ kid culture? Kid culture is perhaps one of the few remaining avenues for possible common dialog and understanding. If nothing else, it often provides a context for connections to the world and sense making in the world. Passion and intrinsic appeal is somehow inherent in kid culture. This dialog and common understanding in kid culture can be used to enhance social education (White 2003). Again, despite the negative view adults often have of various kid culture, there seems little today that we get excited over and that encourages social discourse more so than this culture. Allowing kids to bring in their cultural choices as they investigate issues, make connections, construct knowledge, and engage in sense making may very well be a threat to the entrenched (Daspit and Weaver 2000).

Media literacy must be given credit. It at least enabled the discourse and dialog to be taken seriously. Unfortunately the media literacy movement often has taken the reactionary mind-set to the extreme in assuming its purpose is to ensure the safety of our children. Critically investigating issues of violence, corporate agendas, democracy and citizenship, globalization, information as knowledge, and kid culture as historical fact all should all be part of media efficacy. It should be kid culture for social education. To be sure, the purpose of education should be to enhance critical analysis and problem solving skills; and media efficacy can be integrated to assist in meeting these goals (McLaren 1995).

Shuker suggests several issues regarding kid culture need addressing for teaching and learning purposes (1994). These include the following:

- Economic, market, and consumer issues
- Cultural preferences and social factors
- Ideology, dominance, and agendas
- Kid culture and mass appeal
- Moral panic and kid culture

Perhaps the more intriguing issue regarding kid culture is the idea of moral panic and the "threat" to society. As a result, kid culture is often subject to condemnation, censorship, and regulation. Kid culture has always been questioned regarding its legitimacy and impact on youth and society. Kid culture is often viewed as promoting antisocial behavior and attitudes in youth; therefore, many feel it must be controlled or at the very least ignored (Garofalo 1992). What one often finds in schools is a negative reaction to kid culture in whatever form (rap, Pokemon, video games) through stereotypes, banning, and demeaning acts and comments (White 2003). Much can be said concerning the possibilities of kid culture in promoting social education. And despite the lack of its use in schools, kid culture is a powerful force for social change. Instead of dismissing its potential, schools would be wise to work diligently on integrating kid culture into the teaching and learning process if for no other reason than that there is a desperate need to improve the perceived relevance of schooling (at least in our kids' eyes).

KIDTOONS

One area of kid culture that could easily be integrated into social education is television cartoons. Kids love animation and many cartoons (both old and new) contain ideas, issues, and themes relevant to social education. *Sponge Bob*, one of the most popular kidtoons currently, often deals with social skills development, diversity, and problem solving issues. Japanese anime (*Pokemon, Digemon, Yu-Gi-Oh*) often deals with collaboration, conflict resolution, and problem solving. Allowing kids to engage in projects where they can demonstrate social education through their culture, such as cartoons, would serve as an intrinsic and powerful teaching and learning tool.

Liberty's Kids, Histeria, and *Time Squad* are three cartoons that could be integrated effectively in social education teaching and learning. *Liberty's Kids* and *Time Squad* are presently on television (Cartoon Network and PBS respectively), while *Histeria* reruns are broadcast in a few places. Each cartoon focuses generally on the theme of time, continuity, and change, although other themes such as culture and people, places and environments are certainly integrated.

Liberty's Kids includes the characters Ben Franklin, Sarah Phillips, James Hiller, Henri, and Moses. Through the eyes of two young apprentice reporters named Sarah and James, *Liberty's Kids* engages in adventures in search of the real stories of the American Revolution. Sarah is a British girl right off the ship from England and James, a fifteen-year-old apprentice, sees things from a colonist's perspective. Sarah and James are followed around by eight-year-old Henri, an immigrant from France. Moses, a former slave who freed himself, watches over them for his employer, Benjamin Franklin, with whom we travel to Europe as he fights for recognition and assistance for the young nation.

They meet famous historical figures such as George Washington. Although the setting is colonial America, the characters find themselves in the middle of a revolution that confronts issues that still are current today—gun control, downsizing government, lower taxes, freedom of the press, and race relations. Sample episodes include "The Boston Tea Party," "Intolerable Acts," "United We Stand," "Liberty or Death," and "The Midnight Ride." The website is http://pbskids.org/libertyskids/.

Histeria includes the characters Aka Pella, Big Fat Baby, Charity Bazaar, Father Time, Fetch, and Froggo, among others. The characters in *Histeria,* like those in Time Squad, are not subject to historical barriers and consequently travel throughout history and time, telling the stories in humorous and musical ways. With over fifty episodes titles include "The Wheel of History," "Presidential People," "When America Was Young," and "A Blast from the Past." Particular highlights of *Histeria* are the songs included in each episode. There are many *Histeria* websites; one of the most extensive is www .angelfire.com/tv/enhist.

Time Squad includes three characters, orphan Otto Osworth, robot Larry 3000, and time cop Buck Tuddrussel. These three travel back in time to do whatever it takes to keep history from unraveling. Along the way, the focus is on historical events and people. Often our "heroes" find grand mistakes, bad choices, and unforeseen events affecting famous events or people. It is their job to "save history." Sample episode titles include "Floundering Fathers," "Forget the Alamo," "Where the Buffalo Bill Roams," and "Whitehouse Weirdness." The *Time Squad* website is www.cartoonnetwork.com/ watch/tv_shows/timesquad.

Effective social education suggests powerful approaches that include meaningful, challenging, value-based, integrative, and active teaching and learning. Social education through kid culture and TV cartoons lends itself to facilitating these approaches. Many kids are auditory and visual learners, really interested in animation. Just look at the success of Disney and other animated movies. And look at the success of Cartoon Network, Nickelodeon, anime (*Pokemon, Digemon, Yu-Gi-Oh*), and of course Saturday morning cartoons.

Each of these three series can be applied in social education classrooms in a variety of ways. Snippets of the cartoons can be used to begin a lesson or unit. They can be used to compare and contrast with a more traditional curriculum. Students can use the scripts or cartoons themselves to simulate or role-play events and the actions of famous people. The music and lyrics from *Histeria*, for example, can be integrated for writing and performance activities. Parts or whole episodes can be set up as parts of centers while investigating unit themes, ideas, and issues. Students can be placed in collaborative groups to compare and contrast different cartoons on similar subjects. Students can even use the cartoons to develop their own projects using multimedia, animation software, and other technology. The website of each show contains many opportunities for teaching and learning. *Liberty's Kids* has a particularly useful site for classroom application. The site includes links to educational activities, games, historical connections, plays, and even an online newspaper construction tool.

CENTERS INTEGRATION: HISTORY
(TIME, CONTINUITY, AND CHANGE) THEME

Rationale: We have spent a good deal of time regarding the use of popular culture in teaching and learning and focusing on "powerful" approaches to social studies. Cooperative learning and centers are approaches that facilitate a "powerful" social studies. The purpose of the following centers is to model such integration on the theme of improving popular culture in social studies teaching and learning.

Procedures: In groups of three to four members, rotate through the centers and complete each task. You will be given approximately fifteen minutes in each center. Develop an individual portfolio of materials. When finished you should have evidence of your work for each of the centers. You should also have a group portfolio. The group portfolio should include group sharing notes, group consensus activities, and other "grouped" ideas from each center.

Assessment and expectations: You will have individual content tasks to complete that will contribute to a group task for each center. Each student will keep a portfolio of individual work. All individual and group tasks should focus on developing and sharing "powerful" social studies. Once in groups each person should choose one of the following roles (timekeeper also takes role of on task manager if only three group members):

Timekeeper: Keeps group to fifteen-minute time limit
Reader and materials manager: Reads tasks and ensures understanding
  organizes materials for each center, keeps group materials
Recorder: Takes group notes
On task manager: Ensures that members remain on task at all times

Music

- Choose a song, lyrics, or series of songs from *Histeria*, relevant songs from the period studying, and perhaps the introductory songs from the other cartoons.
- Listen to the song(s) or read the lyrics.
- Have student compare songs using Venn diagrams.
- Have students interpret and analyze the song. What is the song about? What important ideas are presented. How do the lyrics compare to related events?
- Choose a relevant current issue or theme and brainstorm current songs to integrate. Allow students to bring in related songs.

Video

- Watch snippets or episodes from relevant shows.
- Have students take notes or choose most interesting or important parts.
- Have students summarize, critique, and apply the information. Students may write a letter to the editor, develop a newspaper, complete a journal entry, or write a review of the episode as if they were historians.
- Have students create their own scripts and/or videos on related topics or themes.

Simulation

- Have relevant simulation software.
- Decisions, Decisions or Choices, Choices software—Building a Nation, and so on.

- Where in History? Oregon Trail, etc.
- See also Liberty's Kids software.
- Have students engage in related history webquests (http://webquest .sdsu.edu; or (www.ozline.com/learning/index.htm).
- Students can keep reflection/response journals.

Literacy

- Have related primary source and fiction available.
- Allow students to choose a reading to develop an expertise on.
- Develop a newscast from the past or documentary using the sources provided.
- Students should role play relevant people.
- Students could book or source reviews or develop a panel discussion.

Debate

- Choose a controversial issue presented in the episodes (and other sources).
- Develop a pro and con position paper.
- Engage in a debate and/or discussion regarding both sides of the issue.
- Brainstorm positive and negative examples for both sides.
- Complete a reflection paper or project.

Internet

- Explore the cartoon websites:
  http://pbskids.org/libertyskids
  www.angelfire.com/tv/enhist
  www.cartoonnetwork.com/watch/tv_shows/timesquad/
- Allow students to choose games or other interactive area to complete.
- Liberty's Kids (Fun and Games, Behind the Scenes, Liberty Archive, Now and Then, E-Cards, Liberty News)
- Histeria (Episode Guide, Sounds and Songs, Lyrics, Links, Images)
- Time Squad (Episodes, Games)

WHERE TO NOW?

Social education can truly come alive for our kids if we allowed for the integration of kid culture. If we are truly interested in facilitating powerful approaches in social education, then we must begin to integrate long ignored (and often demeaned) tools such as kid culture. What is important is creating a classroom atmosphere where students and teachers are empowered to question and critically analyze social studies issues and themes. Kid culture embodies a language of both critique and possibility; a language that allows students to locate themselves in history, find their own voices, and establish convictions and compassion necessary for democratic civic courage (Freire and Giroux 1989).

Kid culture can be a powerful tool as we hope to develop social education for our students as it allows for transformative investigation. Allowing for the investigation of issues through the tool of kid culture can only enhance powerful teaching and learning. What better way to engage in critical inquiry and problem solving for social education than using kid culture in our classrooms?

REFERENCES

Apple, M., and Beane, J. (1995). *Democratic schools.* Alexandria, VA: ASCD.

Buckingham, D., ed. (1998). *Teaching kid culture.* London: University College/London Press.

Daspit, T., and Weaver, J. (2000). *Kid culture and critical pedagogy.* New York: Falmer.

Freire, P., and Giroux, H. (1989). Pedagogy, kid culture, and public life. In H. Giroux and R. Simon, eds., *Kid culture: Schooling and everyday life.* Granby, MA: Bergin & Garvey.

Garofalo, R., ed. (1992). *Rockin' the boat: Mass music and mass movements.* Boston: South End.

Giroux, H. (1994). *Disturbing pleasures.* New York: Routledge.

McLaren, P., et al. (1995). *Rethinking media literacy.* New York: Lang.

NCSS. (1994). *Expectations for excellence.* Washington, DC: National Council for the Social Studies.

Shuker, R. (1994). *Understanding kid music.* New York: Routledge.

Steinberg, S., and Kincheloe, J. (1997). *Kinderculture: The corporate construction of childhood.* Boulder: Westview.

White, C. (2003). True confessions: Popular culture, social efficacy, and the struggle in schools. Kresskill, NJ: Hampton.

9

Digging *Dead Like Me*

Grrrl Reapers and the (Dis)Embodiments of Feminism

Multimedia technologies, especially visual forms, have often been used to teach history and historical concepts. Often the videos shown in history classes would have little or no audience if not for the students who were unwitting, sometimes unwilling viewers. The blame often can be placed in part on outdated textbook teacher guides that include 16mm films and filmstrips. The widespread availability of films on VHS and DVD seems to have gone relatively unnoticed. However, given the nature of the subject matter of many of the films that are included on these lists, popular movies probably would not be included even in an updated guide. The inclusion of popular television shows is even less likely than popular movies.

Popular movies and television, often maligned by educators, can be equally important teaching tools in a social studies classroom (Walker 2006). Teachers who include popular media in their classroom have a guaranteed hook for their lessons. Beyond its ability to hook students into the learning, popular media can be used to provide engaging critical thinking opportunities for student. Classroom video media libraries are most often filled with non-fiction or documentary films. Generally these films are shown to provide additional facts that students will be required to memorize and subsequently recite. Beyond memorizing facts, the greater learning opportunity with film is the development and exercise of students' critical thinking and concept attainment skills. These skills will provide students with the tools that will allow them to gain a richer understanding of the important concepts that undergird people, places, and events in history.

THEORY TO PRACTICE

There is an almost endless list of popular movies and television shows that contain characters, settings, situations, and so on, that could be used in concept attainment opportunities for students in a social studies classroom. One example of teaching a historical concept through television can be found in using *Dead Like Me* (2003–2004) to teach feminism.

Dead like Me, a "dramedy," a comedy with an occasional dramatic episode or a drama with occasional comedic moments, produced by MGM as an original series on Showtime, was cancelled after two seasons. Information about the series can be found on both the MGM official *Dead Like Me* website and the Showtime official *Dead Like Me* website. Like many television shows, there can be some academic merit in analysis. In the case of *Dead Like Me,* the female grim reapers can be examined to trace the history of feminism in the United States during the twentieth century.

ABOUT THE SHOW

The show is set in contemporary Seattle, although like most of Showtime's original series, it is filmed in Vancouver, British Columbia. The central character (played by Ellen Muth) is Georgia "George" Lass, undead name: Mildred "Millie" Hagen. George was an eighteen-year-old college dropout with a promising future as a temporary file clerk. During a lunch break on her first day of work at the Happy Time Employment Service she was struck and killed by a toilet seat from the Mir space station as it hurtled back to earth. Luckily, or unluckily, depending on your point of view, George's grim reaper, the one who popped her soul just prior to impact by the flaming space debris, completed his quota of souls and moved on. We do not know where he moved on to. Rube comments in one of the episodes that "It's not for us to know" where the deceased go. When George's reaper got his promotion, it left an opening in the violent and/or accidental death division of the greater Seattle grim reaper crew and she was left to fill the spot. This is only one division of grim reapers. There are other reapers who are located in different areas and assigned to many different types of death: plague, old age, and so on. There is also an animal reaper division.

The central premise is that grim reapers walk among us. They look just like everyone else but as grim reapers they appear physically different to the living than they did when they were alive. The living view the reapers differently than when they were alive, or even as they appear to other reapers. Their facial features and body types are rendered unrecognizable to those who might remember them from life. Obviously this becomes less important as time goes by and acquaintances pass on. The job of the grim reapers is to free souls from their bodies just prior to death, so that they are not trapped. This is especially important if that person will die a traumatic, painful, or embarrassing death. Souls that are freed just prior to death suffer no residual effects that they must carry through eternity. Freeing the soul is called "soul popping."

The reapers are given Post-it notes telling them the first initial, last name, address, and ETD (estimated time of death) of everyone who will die. The lack of detail in the Post-it notes sometimes causes mistakes. If a Reaper is late to a reap or there is a case of mistaken identity and a person has already died with soul intact, the reaper must still free the soul; however, the soul will eternally bear the scars, emotional and/or physical, associated with death: autopsy scars, tree limbs protruding from its body, half of a face, and so on. Reapers may feel guilt or anger over their mistakes, but there is no cosmic reprisal. This is not true if a reaper intentionally disrupts the death schedule in some way, as reapers George and Roxie do. In those cases there are serious consequences. Gravelings, or death gremlins, who set the wheels of death in motion will seek retribution on the offending reaper.

There are many other worries for the reapers as well. For one, they do not earn a salary, nor do they receive any sort of assistance from the cosmos; therefore, they must get jobs. Squatting in the newly vacated homes of the recently deceased is acceptable and seemingly encouraged. Taking sentimental personal effects from the dead and grifting the bereaved, however, is frowned on.

There are two men and three women in the Seattle violent death grim reaper group to which George has been assigned. The men are Rube (played by Mandy Patinkin), the boss who died in the early twentieth century, and Mason (played by Callum Blue), a twenty-something slacker who died in the 1960s while attempting to drill a hole in his head to facilitate drug use.

The female characters in *Dead Like Me* are of more interest for the purposes of this discussion. The oldest is Betty Rhomer (played by Rebecca Gayheart), a young a turn-of-the-century adventurer who died in a cliff jumping accident. She is replaced in Episode 5 by Daisy Adair (played by Laura Harris), another young woman who died in the early years of the twentieth century. Daisy was an actress who died from smoke inhalation during a fire on the set of *Gone with the Wind*. Roxanne "Roxy" Harvey (played by Jasmine Guy) is the only African American in the main cast. Roxy is a tough, no-nonsense traffic warden turned police officer (in Season 2). It is often difficult to figure out which job Roxy takes more seriously, writing parking tickets or popping souls. She seems determined to fill her ticket quota before performing a reap or helping a recently departed soul move on. She is also probably the only traffic warden in all of Seattle who carries a sidearm. In Episode 10 viewers are given some insight into Roxy's character. She was murdered in the 1970s by her roommate so that she could steal her new invention: legwarmers. The youngest female reaper is eighteen-year-old "George" Lass. Ironically, George, in her Millie reincarnation, ends up back at Happy Time as a permanent employee. George became a grim reaper and at first was not happy with her new lot in life, or rather death. She had no plan for her life; however, death, or rather undeath, probably was not an obvious alternative. George's transformation required an understandable period of adjustment. She spent the first few episodes coming to grips with her new life, or rather, her new unlife. (I am sure that you get the idea by now, so I will stop using the qualifying "un's.")

These three female characters represent the three distinct periods, or waves, of feminism. These waves are defined by their struggles: the first wave is about legal equality, the second wave, social equality, and the third wave, (popular) cultural equality.

RIDING THE WAVES OF FEMINISM

In the United States, the women's movement of the late nineteenth and early twentieth centuries was predicated on the belief that women should have political equality with men. Key concerns for these first wave feminists were education, employment, marriage laws, and the plight of middle-class single women. They were not primarily concerned with the problems of working-class women, nor did they see themselves as feminists in the modern sense. These first wave feminists mainly were responding to the specific injustices they themselves had suffered. Some of the best known first wave feminists in U.S. history are Emma Goldman, Elizabeth Cady Stanton, and Margaret Sanger.

The central goal of first wave feminism was to gain for women a political voice equal to men. Universal male suffrage had been made a part of the Constitution in 1870 with the Fifteenth Amendment and many women sought a similar constitutionally guaranteed right to vote. In 1920 the Nineteenth Amendment guaranteeing women the right to vote was finally ratified. The Constitution was therefore changed to specifically recognize the legal status of women as voting-eligible citizens of the United States.

Women were recognized as citizens and endowed with those rights and responsibilities; however, this did essentially nothing to effect the unequal positions of men and women in society. Men and even most women were not unhappy with this arrangement. Conceptually this is an important distinction that is often lost on students in our history classes. In the show *Dead Like Me*, Betty, and later Daisy, represent this concept. Both are apparently strong, independent-minded women but both seem squarely placed as women in a world of men. Working for something better but never truly seeming to believe in their absolute equality with men.

The term "second wave" refers to the increase in feminist activity which occurred mainly in the United States and Western Europe from the late 1960s on. In the United States, second wave feminism, often referred to as the women's liberation movement, rose out of the civil rights and antiwar movements in which women, disillusioned with their second-class status even as activists, banded together to fight against discrimination. At 51 percent of the U.S. population in the 1960s, women were hardly a minority group. However, many women experienced sexual discrimination, which was as deeply embedded as racial and ethnic prejudices had been. Economically, while 40 percent of women were in the workforce of 1960, sexual discrimination relegated them to "women's" jobs, such as clerical work, domestic service, retail sales, social work, teaching, and nursing, all of which paid poorly by comparison to men's occupations. Unlike the first wave feminists who primarily concerned themselves with the politics and problems of the middle class, second wave feminists such as Betty Friedan, author of the *Feminine Mystique* (1963), Kate Millett, author of *Sexual Politics* (1969), and Gloria Steinem, founder of NOW, centered their efforts in social, sexual, and work equality for *all* women.

The concept of discrimination is important to a deeper understanding of the second wave of feminism of the 1960s and 1970s. Linked as it was to the civil rights movement, Roxy, the only African American character in the cast of *Dead Like Me*, obviously represents this period. Prior to becoming a reaper, Roxy was a dancer, murdered by her female roommate so that she could claim Roxy's legwarmer invention and realize significant financial rewards. Both Roxy and her murderous roommate were looking for independent economic security. As a reaper, Roxy continues to portray that independent and self-sufficient nature. She is the only reaper with a career rather than a job (traffic warden and later police officer), and the only one who consistently has money. She constantly lectures the other characters, especially George, to be responsible in both money and love. George, of course, has other ideas.

Second wave feminists sought to educate and liberate women as separate and equal. Third wave feminists have abandoned both of these goals and instead are struggling to define themselves in a world where the media and popular culture offer them choices of butch, bitch, or babe. The third wave is returning to pop culture "the medium through which feminism captured the popular imagination—and thus political clout—in the late 1960s and early 1970s" (Orr 1997, 38).

Generally speaking, second wave feminism provides the theory and third wave feminism supplies the action. Schrof (1993) writes, "Where their mothers were accused of being separatists, third wavers are avowed integrationists. Rather than carving out a limited agenda, third wavers want feminism to be an all-encompassing way of life" (p. 70). The challenge for these third wave feminists is to ensure that the world changes to keep up with women's changing roles.

George, the main character in *Dead Like Me*, is a worthy representative of the third wave. While a member of the living community, George drops out of college and seems unable to take an interest in anything, including her own life. She cultivates an air of cynicism that infuriates her mother, baffles her father, and isolates her younger sister. As a reaper, the only change in George is the disappearance of her familial consorts.

She questions and challenges everything. She wants the answers and when they do not suit her, she wants to change the circumstances of the question. She sees more need to change the world than herself. The world according to George and third wave feminists "should be how it should be."

There are indications that in the second (and final) season of *Dead Like Me*, Daisy is moving into fourth wave feminism symbolized by the struggle for religiosity. But that is beyond the scope of this paper and perhaps the show itself given its untimely demise.

CONCLUSION

Concept development through critical thinking skills is an essential component of social studies teaching and learning. Teachers must offer students opportunities to gain this skill. According to the National Council for the Social Studies (1994), social studies teachers should design opportunities for students to increase their abilities to construct new knowledge: "conceptualize unfamiliar categories of information, establish cause/effect relationships, determine the validity of information and arguments, and develop a new story, model, narrative, picture, or chart that adds to the student's understanding of an event, idea, or persons while meeting criteria of valid social studies research."

Multimedia technologies, especially video, can provide students an enticing medium through which to work on these skills. Students will develop skills to "read" movies and television, encouraging them to consider viewing media as an active rather than a passive activity. This will be of use in both academic and life settings. According to the National Council for the Social Studies (1994), "The informed social studies learner applies knowledge and processes from academic disciplines and from interdisciplinary means to both personal and social experiences."

REFERENCES

Bellafante, G., and Chesler, P. (1998). "Is feminism dead?" www.time.com/time/community/transcripts/chattr062598.html.

Dead Like Me. Prod. P. Verschooris. MGM Television.

National Council for Social Studies. (1994). *Expectations of excellence: Curriculum standards for social studies*. Washington, DC: NCSS.

Orr, C. (1997)."Charting the currents of the third wave." *Hypatia* 12(3): 29–45.

Schrof, J. M. (1993). "Feminism's daughters: Their agenda is a cultural sea change." *U.S. News & World Report*, September 27, 68–71.

Verschooris, P. (Producer). (2003–2004). *Dead Like Me*. Hollywood, CA: MGM Television.

Walker, T. (2006). Adventures in Metropolis: Popular culture in social studies. In A. Segall, E. Heilman, and C. Cherryholmes, eds., *Social studies: the next generation: Re-searching in the postmodern*, 171–88. New York: Lang.

10

Give a *Hoot* about *Holes*

Using Recent Youth Culture in Teaching and Learning

Music, movies, technology. and other media can provide powerful teaching and learning tools for connecting with students. Why not use these alternative texts in our classrooms, rather than ignore or censor them? Just look at the quality and success of recent animated movies such a *Shrek, Ice Age, Madagascar,* and *Cars,* for example. Look at the quality of recent children's literature such as Harry Potter or the Lemony Snicket books. We owe it to our students to provide opportunities for integration and critical analysis of youth culture. Film, television, music, books, and other forms of media culture can provide rich opportunities for teaching and learning (Steinberg and Kincheloe 1997). As noted in previous chapters, integrating the popular culture of our youth as a tool in teaching and learning provides needed context and connections for our kids.

Youth culture reflected in movies, books, television, music, media, toys, technology, and fads can be used in a number of ways in education. Again, as stated earlier, the idea of empowering youth with teaching and learning that includes meaningful, challenging, integrative, value-based and controversial, and active approaches should be the goal (NCSS 1994). Youth culture offers a natural integration; just imagine the power of movies, books, television, music, media, toys, technology, and fads in promoting social studies.

Youth culture often provides a context for links to and sense making in the world. Engaging youth culture causes our students' eyes to light up; it encourages a passion often missing in our classrooms. These approaches and integration with youth culture can be used to enhance social studies (White 2003). However, allowing youth to bring in their culture as they investigate issues, make connections, construct knowledge, and engage in sense making may be a threat to the entrenched.

Hoot, by Carl Hiassen, and *Holes*, by Louis Sachar, are two recent examples of youth culture that provided powerful applications for teaching and learning (Hiassen 2002; Sachar 1998). Both began as literature but now have other connections including movies, soundtracks, websites, and other popular culture examples. This chapter explores possibilities for integrating these more traditional texts with other related youth culture texts that have since been developed.

HOOT

Hoot is about three middle school students who challenge land developers, politicians, and other authority figures regarding threats to endangered owls. The book twists and turns among a variety of characters and incidents that focus on change, environmental issues, life skills, and learning.

Hoot offers a great opportunity to engage students in meaningful social studies through youth culture. It allows the context and connections to and for our students often missing in more traditional approaches to social studies. The kids in *Hoot* are kids many of our students (as well as ourselves) can identify with, what with all the youth issues presented in the text and movie. From ideas regarding character, change, friendship, active citizenship, and environmental issues, social studies issues are ripe for inquiry throughout *Hoot*.

The recent movie of the same title and accompanying music soundtrack provide additional resources to promote social studies teaching and learning. In addition to the book, film, and soundtrack, other resources that support the suggested approaches mentioned above include websites, including www.hootmovie.com.

Several social studies themes emerge when using *Hoot* and the accompanying resources. Sample themes that can be integrated at almost any level of social studies include:

Friendship	Interdependence	Adventure
Family	Rights	Perseverance
Rules/Laws	Environment	Trust/Honesty
Cooperation	Character	Consequences
Diversity	Power/Authority	Change
Institutions	Greed	

In addition to the general themes listed above, each of the National Council for the Social Studies ten thematic strands can be addressed with the integration of *Hoot* and the accompanying resources. [8] By integrating the various tools and themes for *Hoot* listed above, we more meaningfully address issues regarding learning styles and real-world connections for our students.

HOLES

Holes, by Louis Sachar, is about Stanley Yelnats, a boy who is plagued by bad luck. After being falsely accused of stealing sneakers, he is sent to a boy's juvenile detention center called Camp Green Lake. Camp Green Lake is no camp, there is no lake, and nothing green has ever grown there. Each day the "campers" dig a hole five feet by five feet, the length and depth of their shovel, and they don't stop until they're finished. The book twists and turns among a variety of characters and incidents that focus on life skills and learning.

Holes offers a great opportunity to engage students in meaningful social studies through media culture. It allows the context and connections to and for our students often missing in more traditional approaches to social studies. Stanley Yelnats is a kid many of our students (as well as we ourselves) can identify with, along with the many youth issues presented in the text and movie. From ideas regarding character, to friendship and history, social studies issues are ripe for inquiry throughout *Holes*.

The recent movie of the same title, and accompanying music soundtrack provide additional rich resources to promote social studies teaching and learning. In addition to the book, film and soundtrack, other resources that support the suggested approaches mentioned above include the book *Survival Guide to Camp Green Lake* and web sites including:

http://disney.go.com/disneypictures/holes
http://falcon.jmu.edu/~ramseyil/sachar.htm
http://www.kidsreads.com/features/010314-holes.asp

Several social studies themes emerge when using *Holes*, and the accompanying resources. Sample themes that can be integrated at almost any level of social studies include:

Friendship	Interdependence	Adventure
Family	Rights	Perseverance
Rules/Laws	Racism	Trust/Honesty
Cooperation	Character	Consequences
Diversity	Power/Authority	
Institutions	Greed	

In addition to the general themes listed above, each of the National Council for the Social Studies ten thematic strands can be addressed with the integration of *Hoot* or *Holes* and the accompanying resources (NCSS 1994). By integrating the various tools and themes for these texts listed above, we more meaningfully address issues regarding learning styles and real-world connections for our students.

INTERMEDIATE/MIDDLE LEVEL SOCIAL STUDIES

In the spring of 2006, I taught a social studies methods course that focuses on student-centered approaches to social studies and asks teachers to think more broadly regarding social studies A group of twenty-four intermediate teachers who were taking a social studies methods course were asked to read the book and see the film *Hoot*. In fall 2006 a similar group was asked to read the book and see the film *Holes*. A primary component of the course is the integration of doing social studies as course projects. These projects include community service, culture fairs, lectures, movies, museums, internships, and the like.

Tied to this approach in the methods class is the idea of integrating a variety of tools to turn kids on to the joys of learning social studies. Youth culture, including movies, music, television, and literature, is promoted as a potentially powerful tool for teaching and learning in the social studies. Rather than imposing our popular culture, the idea is to empower students by allowing them to use their culture to enhance connections in the social studies. As a result, we see the integration of youth culture such as *Sponge Bob, Ice Age, Spiderman, A Series of Unfortunate Events, The Simpsons, Harry Potter, and the Black Eyed Peas.*

This particular project focused on the concept of transdisciplinary social studies, which attempts to be more authentic and integrative toward real-world connections and media culture. The project asked the teachers to compare the book and film, and also summarize, critique, and offer application ideas for the book and film in a narrative. They were also asked to engage in online sharing and discussion regarding their experiences with *Hoot* or *Holes*. Three of the first group of twenty-four teachers had previously read *Hoot*. Six of the second group of twenty-five teachers had read *Holes*.

A rich component of the project included the analysis of the books and films by the teachers regarding social studies issues, ideas, and connections. An interesting debate occurred regarding the themes that were listed in the narratives. Many teachers had difficulty addressing values-based issues such as character, greed, trust, and the like in their classrooms, but they saw these texts as rich opportunities for integrating such themes. More traditional themes such as friendship, change, cooperation, and diversity were also facilitated, according to the teachers. The debate occurred when discussing appropriateness for various grade levels and integration into an already-time consuming and coverage approach curriculum. Teachers often stated that open debate regarding values is frowned on in social studies teaching and learning.

Another strong aspect included the application ideas for social studies teaching and learning. Teachers offered a variety of activities including role playing, reading groups, journal writing, and cooperative learning problem solving. Following is a synthesis of the application ideas placed into a learning center unit format.

Sample Student Comments

"It is refreshing to integrate a variety of texts and tools in my teaching."

"Literature and media really are tools kids can relate to."

"Popular Culture is so cool. It would be a great tool for my teaching."

"Integration of a variety of applications in teaching social studies will really help."

"The project opened up my eyes regarding possibilities for meeting learning style needs."

"Social studies was always so boring. This really opens up your eyes for change."

"I had never heard of this book. It just shows all the possibilities with movies and literature for teaching."

"I am always concerned what the principal or parents might think; but if they only saw the possibilities through this example."

"Using something other than the textbook. What a concept!"

SAMPLE CLASSROOM APPLICATIONS: *HOOT/HOLES* LEARNING CENTERS

Students were asked to include application ideas for using *Hoot* in the social studies classroom. The following includes the synthesis of project ideas shared developed into a learning center unit.

Rationale: Integrating youth culture and focusing on powerful teaching and learning including active, challenging, meaningful, values-based, and integrative approaches can enhance social studies education. Cooperative learning and centers are examples of strategies that enhance a powerful"social studies. The purpose of the following centers is to model the integration of youth culture in social studies teaching and learning. Each of the ten NCSS thematic strands is addressed in this project.

Procedures: In groups of three to four members, rotate through the centers and complete each task. Develop an individual portfolio of materials. When finished, you should have evidence of your work for each of the centers. You should also have a group portfolio. The group portfolio should include group sharing notes, group consensus activities, and other grouped ideas from each center.

Assessment and expectations: You will have individual content tasks to complete that will contribute to a group task for each center. Each student will keep a portfolio of individual work. All individual and group tasks should focus on developing and sharing powerful social studies. Once in groups each person should choose one of the following roles (timekeeper also takes role of on task manager if only three group members):

Timekeeper: Keeps group to negotiated time limit

Reader and materials manager: Reads tasks and ensures understanding organizes materials for each center, keeps group materials

Recorder: Takes group notes

On task manager: Ensures that members remain on task at all times

Hoot/Holes: The Books

Have students read the books. (This can be down as a comparison unit or using only one of the texts.) Initial strategies should include teacher read aloud and whole class focus activities. Reading centers could be set up for small group reading, book discussion groups, literacy sets, and comprehension and extension activities. Have students summarize, critique, and apply ideas and issues from the book in the reading center. A reading reflection journal could be used.

Music

- Choose a song, lyrics, or series of songs from the soundtracks.
- Listen to the song(s) or read the lyrics.
- Have students compare songs using Venn diagrams or other method.
- Have students interpret and analyze the songs. What are the songs about? What important ideas, issues, and themes are presented?
- Choose a relevant current issue or theme and brainstorm current songs to integrate. Allow students to bring in related songs.

Film/Video

- Watch the films or snippets from the films.
- Have students take notes or choose most interesting or important parts.

- Have students summarize, critique, and apply the information. Students may write a letter to the editor, develop a newspaper, complete a journal entry, write a review of the film as if they were historians.
- Have student create own scripts and/or videos on related topics or themes.
- Have students compare the film with other films of interest.

Literacy Connections

- Have related primary sources and fiction available (*Survival Guide to Camp Green, Small Steps, Over the Hedge*).
- Have students read the book.
- Develop a comic strip, letter to the editor, reading reflection journal.
- Students should present their projects creatively.

Debate

- Choose a controversial issue presented in the books/films (and other sources).
- Develop a pro and con position paper.
- Engage in a debate and/or discussion regarding both sides of the issue.
- Brainstorm positive and negative examples for both sides.
- Complete a reflection paper or project.

Technology

- Explore the appropriate websites and/or DVD extras:
  http://www.hootmovie.com
  http://www.holes.com
  http://disney.go.com/disneypictures/holes
- Allow students to choose relevant areas to explore.
- Students should keep a web journal of their exploration.

Hoot/Holes Project

- Groups should choose a theme/issue addressed in *Hoot/Holes*.
- Students should develop a history fair type of project on the theme as addressed in *Hoot/Holes* and applied to a current relevant topic or issue.
- Possible projects include a skit/oral project, visual project, video project, or technology project (or a combination or other project as negotiated).
- Projects will be completed in the center and presented to whole class.

Extensions

Another recent possible example of youth culture is the film *Over the Hedge*. Much like *Hoot* and *Holes*, there are a variety of texts for classroom integration and comparison. Themes in *Over the Hedge* include development, animal rights, and environmental protection. The film is based on the comic trip of the same name. The official comic website is www.comics.com/comics/hedge. This offers links to archived comics, books, and other possible resources. The film website is www.overthehedge-movie.com. Once again, this is interactive with a variety of links and activities tied to themes from the film, including games, the movie trailer, and music. The film also has a very topical music soundtrack that can also be used.

GIVING A *HOOT* ABOUT *HOLES*

Learning can truly come alive for our students if we allow for the integration of youth culture. If we are truly interested in facilitating student-centered approaches in social studies, then we must begin to integrate long ignored (and often demeaned) tools such as media culture. What is important is creating a classroom atmosphere where students and teachers are empowered to question and critically analyze social studies issues and themes. Youth culture embodies a language of both critique and possibility; a language that allows students to locate themselves in history, find their own voices, and establish convictions and compassion necessary for democratic civic courage (Freire and Giroux 1989).

Youth culture can be a powerful tool as we hope to develop social studies for our students as it allows for critical inquiry and investigation. Allowing for the investigation of issues through the tool of media culture can only enhance an engaging social studies education. *Hoot* and *Holes* are only two examples of many that deserve further investigation regarding the potential for engaging kids more effectively. What better way is there to engage in critical inquiry and problem solving for teaching and learning than using youth culture in our classrooms?

REFERENCES

Daspit, T., and Weaver, J. (2000). *Kid culture and critical pedagogy.* New York: Falmer.

Freire, P., and Giroux, H. (1989). "Pedagogy, kid culture, and public life." In H. Giroux and R. Simon, eds., *Kid culture: Schooling and everyday life.* Granby, MA: Bergin & Garvey.

Hiassen, C. (2002). *Hoot.* New York: Knopf.

National Council for the Social Studies. (1994). *Expectations for excellence.* Washington, DC: NCSS.

Sachar, L. (1998). *Holes.* New York: Dell Yearling.

Steinberg, S., and Kincheloe, J. (1997). *Kinderculture: The corporate construction of childhood.* Boulder: Westview.

White, C. (2003). *True confessions: Popular culture, social efficacy, and the struggle in schools.* Kresskill, NJ: Hampton.

11

Films for the Times

Using the Three Versions of *Invasion of the Body Snatchers* for Teaching Postwar America

What if a teacher could demonstrate that one single motif integrates the past fifty years of U.S. history in a way that students find enjoyable, provocative, and accessible? Of the various ways high schools attempt to teach postwar America, many focus on the organic link between the bombing of Hiroshima, the cold war, the Vietnam War 1960s cultural politicizations 1970s recovery 1980s Reaganism, and 1990s multiculturalism and globalization movements. This is not a bad way to go, focusing the students' minds on the exponential existences that factor into history; getting them to see links like these helps them to see their own futures as exigent (Hope 1995). Perhaps they may then take some caution in their paths. But what if we could get them to see links between cause and effect, between past and present (and thus future), even with respect to the march of time, without the need to move forward through history as the only way to study history?

Students often respond best when they both see a relevance to the learning and make implicit connections to it themselves (Brooks and Brooks 1993). Breaking up the process, allowing students to learn differently than simply by chapter to chapter (nothing wrong with using the text . . . unless that is all you are using) provides a less stable but more open emphasis. Not keeping abreast in this method or working contextualizing their own understandings of the material often presupposes students to failure. But acceptance of and participation in this method has the added reward of making history a continual event, a constant, requiring active reexamination. History for the students thus becomes what they make of it. It can live if they choose it to, since they are becoming the keepers (and hopefully the makers) of the myths. Or it can die because they deem it must.

Giving students that power requires showing them how history always has and will be under a microscope (Loewen 1995). Not that facts change, but our appreciation of the facts, those past events we have tweaked with scholarship, has. And what better way to do this than by using perhaps the most powerful medium of the twentieth century: film. Because many perennialist educators abhor the intrusion of this resource into the classroom, most teachers use it reluctantly at best. When they do, often neither they nor the students understand the role it can play. Instead, film is offered as a respite from "real" learning, a vehicle for time maintenance (or passage) and/or gestalt effect: the hope that students will remember the subject simply because they saw a film about it. Thus film plays little critical cognitive role in the classroom, and teachers who see their roles as progenitors of cognitive development rarely use the medium.

Yet students do respond to film as a teaching tool, if only because of its rarity and its difference, its presence *and* its absence. Film possesses a magical power to naturalize events for students in a way that books or lectures cannot; if it is on film, it happened. Building on this, part of presenting history in film concerns how to use film critically, cognitively, and specifically as a resource devoted to fostering higher-level thinking. Students can be shown to look at film as metaphor, as distortion, and as a resource. Taking students to the raw facts, leading them through a discussion on implications of the events, and exposing them to the art of criticism all pave the way for a lesson in film that does not simply become a free day (Wilson and Herman 1994).

Film can become the crux of the learning, but not all the learning. Just as any educator has more than one method to revive students' minds, so too with film. Using it in conjunction with articles, essays, research, role-playing, and writing exercises expands the students' conception of learning (and keeps them from deadly stasis). The key, however, is finding the balance of these discourses while still making the film the centerpiece of the lesson. Shifting into context, the students begin to see links between thoughts and words, images and perceptions, even perhaps entertainment and news. And the past fifty years of American history has seen a revelatory explosion in this last dialectic. While many films do cover these various themes (among others, also successfully) of postwar America, most continue to affirm the idea of history as separate events (no matter how successfully those organic links are made and no matter how committed one may be to teaching history as a collection of disbursals). But what if we had one film that brought all distinct themes of this era together?

One film (rather, a series of the same film) achieves this objective. *Invasion of the Body Snatchers* came out in 1958, was remade in 1978, and then redone again, as *The Body Snatchers*, in 1993. Each remake retains the central plot and fear of the pod people, but establishes its own distinct subtext, dovetailing nicely into a reconstitution of its historical era. Because these films duplicate fears but imbue them with differing historical significance, the students get both a historical imperative and an art history lesson. Feed students the opportunity to find the difference themselves, let them dissect the films with their own eyes, and maybe knowledge becomes more than stale facts. Maybe they can connect for themselves the changes in our nation's culture by analyzing a reoccurring theme. Students need some prepping to understand what they are looking for in the films.

THE 1950s

For the 1950s, several sources provide a comprehensive and engaging read. While many state-mandated texts are bereft of the full extent of the history of the rise and threat of communism in America (with all its various incarnations and red scares), they cover the content enough to give the students basic background information. For better detail, use Eric Goldman's *The Crucial Decade and After: 1945–1960* or David Halberstam's opus, *The Fifties.* (The History Channel has converted David Halberstam's book to video.) Asking them to compare these sources primes them for analysis is the very thing they will need when watching the film.

Start with excerpts from Eric Goldman's *The Crucial Decade.* Telling the postwar history of America in narrative style, the book personalizes the actors and their actions. Select the sections of the book that best provides students scaffolding for understanding the era. Because the book limns almost all of the events from 1945 (V-J day) to 1960 in a mythic timeline, it can fill in gaps in student understanding. The book takes particular care to depict McCarthy as an atavistic opportunist, and his era itself as a moral struggle for the New Deal idealists against the free enterprise reactionaries depicted as conservatives. Or vice versa.

Since individual teachers know their students best—their prior knowledge, their rate and capability of comprehension, their retention and effort—each teacher should glean the sections most appropriate for his or her own teaching. In order to get the students to access this information post reading, ask them some higher-level questions about the events. The best questions are the Why? and What would you do? types that require students to get inside the psychology of the character or the event. These encourage the students to actually be historians by doing something with their learning besides just memorizing. They also allow students to answer without feeling they must come up with the right answer as their teacher would define it. This freedom to present their answer/idea/opinion involves them as learners and, implicitly, as historians. Discussing the readings, either in conjunction with these questions or in lieu of them, can also encourage the students to use the knowledge and to defend their theories. Because the panics inspired by communism derive from such a broad picture, using these question sessions can help to gauge the basic knowledge base of the students. Include more sections from the texts if necessary in developing better background knowledge.

A teacher might also use the Halberstam/History Channel rendition of *The Fifties* judiciously to focus on McCarthy. Although it excludes much of the periphery to the red scare, the episode on Tail Gunner Joe is specifically tailored to show how brutal his effect was. Interviews with State Department analysts whose careers he affected (and the effects on our foreign policies) or with several reporters who watched his rise give the era a distinctly personal "you are there" touch. Again, asking the students to put themselves in each participant's head, including McCarthy's, can make this much more meaningful. Sample questions might include:

Why do you think he did what he did?
Was he right to do what he did? Why or why not?
Was he a hero or a villain? Why?

A teacher can also have them compare the two sources.

Which do you find more explicit?
More believable?
More persuasive?
Why?

Having to take these positions starts the students on the task of analyzing what is present but unsaid. It asks them to find for themselves the answers instead of repeating what someone has told them. One can even get them to grade each others' analyses as a way of making them more responsible in defending their own views.

Showing the 1950s version of the film should be the next step. Demonstrating their ability to pick out the subtext should be central to the lesson. Exposing students to reviews beforehand may encourage them to simply adapt these ideas without assembling them themselves. A strategy would be to ask them to prepare a critical analysis of the film as a document of the history of the decade. Possible questions for this analysis include:

What, from what we have recently studied, do you see in the film? Give examples.
What is the message of the film?
How does this message relate to the history we have studied?
How effective is the film at sending this message?

What group of society does the protagonist represent? Explain.
Who or what do the pod people represent? Explain.
Who or what do the pods represent? Explain.
Is there a difference between the two? Explain.
Who/what does Miles represent? Explain.

Since each teacher knows his or her students best, questioning strategies should be personalized; the only caveat is to not allow the students to be too literal with the film. It is important for them to avoid using the overt narrative as the message, which only reinforces their penchant for seeing things as depicted, and not searching for the engine or message behind the depiction. Get them to dig deeper in their interpretive skills to prove their point. After this assignment, a discussion of student ideas with the entire class should occur. Open up the dialog to let others comment on and debate the merits of various interpretations. It is also vital to remind them that every theory is valid as long as it is accompanied by persuasive writing and reasoning; the students should feel efficacy in comparing their ideas with others.

THE 1970s

The 1970s are more diffuse to cover, perhaps because we are still recovering from this decade. Although if the recent rage in retro clothes means anything, our facility for deconstructing the decade is growing sharper (first the clothes, then the culture, then the politics, then deconstructing the deconstruction). To start, take on cultural politics instead of governmental intrusion; focus on this version of the film as a critique of the creeping conformity (also a mainstay of McCarthyism) that the me-decade thrust at us, and its ambient lure of self-help, self-interest, self-improvement, self-selfism.

A teacher could start with Michael Lewis's personal account of the madness of the Wall Street world, *Liar's Poker*. Using a first-person style, he chronicles the obliviousness of the decade from inside the culture that spawned a multi-billion-dollar breakdown in our financial institutions (the 1980s savings and loan scandal on top of the country's deficit spending). *Liar's Poker* jumps into the heart of the decade's acculturation of greed and reactionism. Spawned by the same type of reaction that made the 1950s such a response to the New Deal of the 1930s, the 1970s created a generation so intent on denying their own causations that they sublimated the radicalization of the 1960s into a fixation on accumulation.

Michael Lewis gives as good a depiction of these times in his book. Its first-person account of life as a Wall Street player shows the personalities evenhandedly; they are neither glamorized nor criticized—they just . . . are.

This style, like Goldman's, keeps the reading light, swift, and enjoyable, especially for students who have come to regard history as stale, dry, boring, lifeless, needless, ad nauseum. As with the Goldman reading, use selections you think will capture your students' attention. The section on the bond traders and the one on Lewis's own socialization into this world demonstrate the lesson precisely because each refuses to make apologies for the era or its participants. Lewis simply shows *what it was like* . This is the kind of reading students need to experience to see how history (learning!) is life itself.

A teacher might focus the students on the end of the Vietnam War, the end of the civil rights decade, the beginning of the conservative movement and the start of globalization. The text always comes in handy for background knowledge. Also, use *Cadillac Desert* by Marc Reisner. It shows Carter's attempts to reclaim the country's mind-set on continuing the 1960s neoliberalism. More specific than the other sources cited so far, this book goes after the folly of America's water policy. Reisner's chapter on Carter gives a great description on how liberalism got smashed, in the person of the Democratic president. This rather lengthy chapter chronicles the idealism Carter had at the outset of his tenure in office. Readers can then watch how the forces of reactionary conservatism bled the pragmatism out of him.

Add Tom Wolfe's *In Our Time*, a witty, weighty attack on 1970s culturalism. Loaded for bear, the book comes overstuffed for most high school students, but you could choose the essay that best fulfills your needs and help your class wade through it. For a social view of the decade, Tom Wolfe makes a terrific source. (In fact, more of his writings can be found throughout issues of the leading source of cultural consciousness from the 1970s, *Rolling Stone* magazine.) Use his words as a counterbalance to Lewis's financial mind-set or Reisner's political criticism, and to show how creeping conformity caused people to go to extremes to fit their own personalities into this era. Choosing the selections that allow you to show the students examples of 1970s thinking (you are the best arbiter of your own students' interests), get the students to compare the styles and messages of these three writers.

> How do the events in one seem to represent the themes in the other?
> Which source is more opinion?
> Why?
> Does that make it any less valid?
> Why or why not?

In order to focus on understanding the people of this era, next try letting the students create a short play about the era. (Working in groups on this short-term project tends to move them more efficiently to finish the task. Especially with you there as a guiding resource.) Ask them to include financial, political, and social issues in their story line. Now that they have been exposed to the idea of subtext from your discussions of the 1958 version of the film, remind them to try (and stress try) to incorporate some message into the actions of their characters that show what they (the student writers) think about the era. This will not only give them a creative outlet; it will also show them that entertainment must have a comment on the subject it shows. And it will prepare them to pick out from the 1978 version of the film what its director/writer/producer was trying to say about the decade. Before showing them the film, ask your students to write a review from their two favorite movies. Have other students grade the reviews on persuasiveness, writing (grammar, spelling, etc.), and creativity (How enjoyable did you find this review?). Then, require them to bring in at least three different reviews from any sources of these films. Have them compare these professional reviews with their own and critique themselves on criteria such as:

What makes the reviews different?
Which is most persuasive? Why?
Which is the best (their definition)? Why
How would they improve these reviews?

Now get them to rewrite their reviews, based on their classmates' comments and their exposure to these reviews.

Now you can show the students the 1978 version of the movie after the readings. Ask the students to both pick out the trends and fears they have just read about, but also to contrast the film with the first. Here are some questions to have them consider:

How is the central character depicted?
How different is his reaction to the pod people?
What do the pod people represent in each film?
How is the film evocative of the era?
Which version makes its message most clearly? How?
Why did the second film change?
What effect did the changes have on its message?
How do these changes show the changes in society? Be specific.

THE 1990s

To prepare for the last film, prompt the students to list the important historical events that have occurred during their lifetime. Take them to the library to research important dates (their specificities) and events that link important stages in their histories. Cultural and social events might make the transition to this era more palpable if only because the students have a greater sense of trends than they do of politics. But try to focus their minds on the major issues that have arisen in this decade: environmentalism, multiculturalism, the soaring economy, or even education-based issues they feel strongly about (standardized tests, social promotion, uniforms, violence et al.) Readings from *The Nation*, the *New Yorker*, *Rolling Stone*, *Spin*, *Wired*, or *Mondo*, or even *Time* and *Newsweek* on contemporary society would make great tangents to place recent events in a quasi-historical context. This process helps students see even their own era as integral to shaping history and the world's ideological makeup. While they are engaged in this research, hold a discussion among your students about how they get their information, how they express their opinions, and how they would compare their era with the two they just studied. (Even start a working list of sources for you to go to in order to grasp their take on the world.)

What are the similarities?
What are the differences?
How would you show the differences?
What would you focus on to show how things have changed?
Have the changes been for the good or the bad? Give examples.
How would you show this?

Michel Foucault stressed the inability of one age to survey its own time (what he called its "archive") (Popkewitz and Brennan 1998). Call it the philosophical uncertainty principle; it is still necessary, however, to help students understand that they must be thinking, critical beings if they want to take control of their lives. They may be cynical, apathetic, and unmotivated, but they do interact with the forces of culture and society. Use this section of the curriculum to engage students in a discussion (even if metacognitive, actually—*especially* if metacognitive) about what it means to be a part of the world around them. But instead of bringing readings about the nature of being, and needlessly depressing the more attuned, require them to create for you a cross-section of their lives. As a short-term research project (best started best before you enter this extended lesson and built into their research about their dates and their generation's role in history), require that they begin compiling readings about their culture, their era that they think best depicts who they are, what it means to be them. Give them wide latitude to interpret their times as broadly, specifically, and personally as they need. Have them create a journal, book, or portfolio with a collection of five to ten articles, images, readings, music/television/movie reviews, art, or whatever they feel adequately shows in the public sphere what it means to live in this age. Once these are due, have a museum-like display, as if your students are the curators of their era. Invite other classes, parents, teachers, friends, enemies, pets, whoever, to come and view the students' projects. And invite the guests to respond to particular exhibits with notes, messages, or letters.

Afterward, get the students to share the responses they received. Hold a town hall discussion among your students about each other's work. Generate a general synopsis for what their views are on this era (reminding them that everyone who came to see their work, every classmate, everybody *alive* is also part of their archive and has as valid an interpretation of their world as the students do), creating an ongoing list of adjectives, images, or notions. Instead of bringing in outside readings, ask the students to choose several isolated images and/or views from their classmates to write about.

Why are there so many different views?
What are some similarities?
Do you agree with some views of one student but disagree with his or her other views?
Why is that?

Once students are cognizant of their generation's impact in/on history, show the most recent film version. Again, allow them to write about the film in empirical terms, and then in comparison to the others. Assign them a formal essay asking them which film most persuasively allegorizes its era and why. Continue the writing exercises from earlier, but include questions that get the students to comment on the archives they have created, including questions the students may have brought to you about the films and their meanings. Focus them on comparing the film's version of their lives with their own versions of their lives. Students might be tired of the images or they might be emboldened by the varying texts the film exposes. Have them prepare a film treatment where they create a new version of the film, complete with a subtext they think best exemplifies the tensions and fears of their contemporary society. Share these ideas with the class at large. For a finale, ask students to write a comprehensive paper, not on how films comment on their era but on how accurately films comment on their era. Encourage the students to be skeptical and critical and cynical. Use their own strengths in a constructive way. Present the purpose of the paper as an analysis of the way society depicts history and how this depiction is consumed. They might understand, when forced to play historian, that history is simply myth, reconstituted from the personal opinions of the author to be accepted as truths by the readers (or viewers in this lesson).

CONCLUSION

The more the students write, they more they learn, because they are forced to comprehend the material in a way that allows for them to make their own connections and contextualizations. And writing about films helps them to see everything they experience in the world as potential for critique. Once they make the connection to how their views on something as arbitrary as film are as applicable to their views on the world itself, then perhaps they will take a more critical, less knee-jerk cynical approach to life (Giroux 1994). Films allow them to see art as more than a commercial exercise. They will be consumers all their lives; maybe with a little push, they will circumspect consumers. And perhaps they will become more tuned in citizens.

While some students will be reluctant to do much of this, precisely because they do not see what facts are to be learned (and thus without value, reason, or use), your job is not to worry about these aberrations. The purpose of this curriculum is to give students a chance to analyze history not as a dry allotment of facts and dates, but as an ongoing critique of their own era. Students' appreciation for this fact may not arrive until later, perhaps much, much later. And many may personally swear off movies if they think they have to approach them reverently. But this lesson gives them a chance to see that everything around them is in some way a reaction to, and a dialog with, the world. They too have that responsibility. And meanwhile, they get to watch a film for meaningful learning.

REFERENCES

Brooks, J., and Brooks, M. (1993). *The case for constructivist classrooms.* Alexandria, VA: Association for Supervision and Curriculum Development.

Eisner, M. (1986). *Cadillac Desert.* New York: Viking.

Foucault, M. (1972). *Archaeology of knowledge.* New York. Pantheon.

Giroux, H. (1994). *Disturbing pleasures.* New York: Routledge.

Goldman, E. (1971). *The crucial decade—And after.* New York: Knopf.

Halberstam, D. (1993). *The '50s.* New York: Villard.

Invasion of the Body Snatchers–1956, Director–Don Siegel, Walter Wagner Productions.

Invasion of the Body Snatchers–1978, Director–Philip Kaufman, Solofilm.

Invasion of the Body Snatchers–1978, Director–Abel Ferrara, Warner Brothers.

Lewis, M. (1989). *Liar's poker.* New York: Norton.

Loewen, J. (1995). *Lies my teacher told me.* New York: Touchstone.

Reisner, M. (1986). *Cadillac desert.* New York: Viking.

Popkewitz, T., and Brennan, M., eds. (1998). *Foucault's challenge: Discourse, knowledge, and power in education.* New York: Teachers College Press.

Wilson, W., and Herman, G. (1994). *American history on the screen.* Portland, ME: Walch.

Wolfe, Tom. (1980). *In our time.* New York: Farrar, Straus, Giroux.

12

The Message in the Music

Using Current Music to Connect Social Studies

> Songs are able to reach deep down inside the listener. This is the highest form of musical expression, where the music is not merely listened to but felt.

> —Flaska 2000

Music is the universal language, or so the saying goes. Most people love music and may even find solace as they listen to their preferred musical genres. How often do songs "take us back" to a memory long past? Because music can evoke deep personal meanings, social studies educators often use songs to emphasize larger historical moments. This personalization phenomenon continues as today's youth explore their own musical genres and store today's memories. Because music is a vital component of youth's popular culture preferred over even movies and television (Rideout, Roberts, and Foehr 2005), the teacher's understanding and application of popular music can be a powerful tool for teaching and learning in social studies education. Yet, like other forms of popular culture, the role of contemporary popular music in schooling is minimal. The educator's reluctance to use music may reflect a disconnect between students' lives and teachers' understanding of their world.

Popular music is seldom used as a text in social studies education outside of looking at musical genres through history, a practice illustrated by the increasing number of suggestions for integrating music in the social studies (Harris 2004; Bafumo 2004; Palmer 1998). This is a start, but music's full potential is underutilized, especially that of contemporary popular music. As social studies educators, we face the challenge of providing students with tools that critically examine relevant societal issues and allow us better tools for bridging connections to their worlds; current popular music is a way to do just that. However, our traditional social studies education is so entrenched with covering essential knowledge to ensure high test scores, that excuses are often used for not integrating current music. Teachers do not have enough time, popular music is inappropriate, it is not relevant, or there is just a lack of knowledge. If we are interested in a relevant social studies that facilitates active participation and problem solving in society, then contemporary popular music offers many possibilities and can play a vital role in instruction.

What with the myriad of social problems at present, meaningful integration of current issues in teaching and learning is often difficult. Many educators find it difficult to examine serious social problems confronting a significant number of students such as poverty, racism, abuse, addiction, and global issues such as hunger, disease, and war. Following in the footsteps of earlier entertainers, today's artists like the Black Eyed Peas, Dixie Chicks, and Green Day focus on these social issues that should be allowed entrance into our classrooms. Through lyric explorations, music is a tool that opens tremendous opportunities for social studies educators to begin meaningful conversations about these issues and connect with students. Part of our responsibility as educators is to analyze the historical role that music plays in this endeavor, but more important, to use these examples to connect to the struggles that are waged now.

OUR STORIES

Coincidentally, we both first stumbled on this as we began our careers as eighth grade American history teachers diligently plugging away at the prescribed curriculum using district approved textbooks and ancillaries. In a never-ending attempt to engage students, we even tried more creative strategies such as simulations and cooperative learning. Our early teaching experiences were similar in the shared realization that we achieved little success in making connections with a majority of students in either classroom setting. We became increasingly disillusioned and knew that changes had to be made, but how? We both knew that if we wanted to ensure that students learn the material that we would have to challenge them through active learning. While students often seemed unwilling to participate, the real problem rested with our inability to make the content engaging—students were unable to make personal meanings with the material. Fortunately we both have powerful stories in which our students provided the push that created an epiphany regarding the potential of contemporary popular music in teaching and learning.

The first experience began midway through the inaugural semester as Susan introduced the series of acts and other historical events prior to the American Revolution. My eighth grade students demonstrated a determined resistance for learning. Perplexed by their blatant challenge, I was unable to connect with students despite using pedagogical tools which may only be associated with novice educators—translation, traditional pedagogy. On a morning drive to work, a catchy little tune played on the radio. Mentally running through the list of events to cover during that day's lesson, I had an inspiration: I would change the lyrics of the song to reflect the events leading up to the Boston Tea Party—"The Roof, the roof, the roof is on fire!" became "The tea, the tea, the tea was in the harbor" (Bloodhound Gang 1996). The factual information was now connected to a popular rap/rock song, "Fire, Water, Burn," with which most of the students were familiar.

After careful reflection there were two results; the students gained new respect for me because I integrated a song to reflect their popular culture, and they responded enthusiastically during the rest of what, in retrospect, was merely a lesson designed to promote memorization of historical facts and dates. Students were sorted into groups and equipped with their very own historical event, expected to conduct basic research and rewrite songs that would explain their acts. Former resisters created outstanding performances enjoyed by audience and artists alike demonstrated by subtle body movements during each group's demonstration.

There are two crucial points to consider. First, Susan realized that students' interests were not previously considered, and music helped bridge that gap. Unfortunately, the second point exposes the reality that this exercise was little more than facts-based memorization with an aesthetic flair.

Another story found Cameron frustrated by overreliance on traditional chronological and fact-based approaches in American history. Historical folk music was introduced in an attempt to illustrate the connections between issues, struggles, and conflict as ongoing themes throughout history. While the students temporarily appreciated the change in focus and the integration of music, many still had problems with the content, as they found it difficult connecting to my personal musical choices. However, an interesting conversation began as one student asked me to consider Pink Floyd's "The Wall" (1987):

Another brought up selections by early rap groups such as GrandMaster Flash's "The Message" (2005).

The remainder of the year found music of historical times integrated with current music as tools to compare similar issues in a variety of units; subsequent projects integrated student generated music selections. Students connected similar messages we were studying in American history such as conflict, change, and rights. The novelty of music opened the door

for communication, but more contextualized teaching and learning of social studies occurred only when students where encouraged to speak
through the messages in their music. This led to the ongoing integration of
music in most social studies units as we explored common themes across
time. This was only the first step of a long journey.

ISSUES AND IDEAS

Forging the way for all social studies educators, a few educators have been
instrumental in setting the stage for the type of critical learning possible in
a classroom infused with music. Responding to growing social diversity,
music allows other voices not related to the dominant culture to emerge. In
his article "Middle Schoolers and the Blues," Harris (2004) explains how he
uses blues to appeal to a population of students who continue to be marginalized in history textbooks, only one of today's important social com-
mentaries. Most recent music genres and many individual contemporary
artists include examples of songs that contain social commentary or historical references.

Many people assume that social commentary in music reached its pinna-
cle in the late 1960s and early 1970s. Founded in the 1980s, punk, hip-hop,
rap, grunge, and alternative continue to provide considerable social commentary and historical references. Traditional rock still has much to say regarding social efficacy and activism. And these are often the genres that
most interest youth. While we may not understand or like the music of today, we cannot blindly dismiss its potential for critical social efficacy and
activism. Remember the struggles from early folk and rock days.

Through its history, popular culture, like all forms of media, has not only
reflected the times but impacted the times and served as a catalyst for critical social inquiry and societal change. Music can be a powerful theme as we
investigate issues such as ethnicity and the struggle for equality, population
growth, economics, technology, business and industry, efficacy, and empowerment within the context of social history (Szatmary 2000).

The impact that music plays on those who identify with its popular elements is hard to ignore, but is readily dismissed by others who claim that
popular culture has no real significance to society's development. Rosenthal
(1998), reporting on his experience of teaching music and social movements at Wesleyan University, debates music's function and whether or not
it actually helps any social movement. He claims that movements do not
need music to be successful, and, conversely, music needs no movement to
be popular. However, he insists that his students gain much needed media
literacy by examining critical issues inherent in popular or contemporary
music.

Today's youth should struggle with issues like the deterioration of family, drug abuse, and violence—themes frequently explored in popular music. But these issues are not isolated to one ethnic population; they transcend all ethnic lines. The same messages are demonstrated when the band System of a Down addresses social issues in many of their songs such as "Shimmy." "Education, subjugation, now you're out, Go./ Indoctrination, of a nation,/ Indoctrination of a nation,/ Subjugation of damnation,/ Subjugation of damnation?"

Other issues the band addresses include war and inhumanity. Today's artists recognize broad ranging societal ills and their influence on our youth. Isn't it time that educators recognize them as well? Our acceptance of their impact and willingness to introduce them in our teaching and learning would serve as the catalyst for critical communication and possibly future activism. A number of artists including John Mayer include topical themes in recent work.

If the messages are meant to galvanize today's youth, many popular artists criticize student passivism. Do all artists take on the role of activist? Bob Dylan once remarked that "there's other things in this world besides love and sex that're important" (Szatmary 2002). He would encourage an entire generation to reject racism and other social evils to make a difference regardless of youthful appearance. This philosophy would not be embraced by the dominant culture, nor would it be the last time that the establishment would try to disparage popular artists. Nevertheless, perhaps because of global issues, artists are increasingly willing to maneuver their way into social controversy, such as Micael Franti in "Yell Fire."

Green Day (Hendrickson 2004) counters this position with an album called *American Idiot*, which is a criticism of current U. S. global policies. Does youth understand the artist's intended message? Some would argue that popular artists like this have a duty to the public. Arundhati Roy suggests that "a great writer may refuse to accept any responsibility or morality that society wishes to impose on her. Yet the best and greatest of them know that if they abuse this hard-won freedom, it can only lead to bad art" (2001, 5). Despite this imposed duty, will our students respect the artists' attempts? Roy realizes the duty to the public and the importance of separating "the strong, true, bright bird of the imagination from the synthetic, noisy bauble" (2001, 6). What is important to remember is that what one culture deems bright and imaginative is a cacophony of incoherence to another. Today's youth most likely recognizes the artists who focus on authentic movements. Some express their skepticism in the artists who support causes on a whim. As social studies educators, we have to work with students through media literacy to explore and support a variety of interpretations.

Raymond Horn (2003) charges educators with the duty to assist students as they began to decipher the messages in the media and develop a critical awareness of what they are consuming. Broad themes like oppression and hegemony may be hidden within the lyrics, but students may not have developed an adequate "media literacy" that allows them to participate in projects at that critical level. As students transition between simply listening to music for enjoyment to critiquing the artists' messages, there are ample opportunities for meaningful connections, but only if the educator is willing to translate the popular culture into the dominant culture's terminology. This will require students to perform at higher cognitive levels than expected on standards based curriculums, but epitomizes education that is aimed at teaching democratic values.

Who should decide the messages to present? One history teacher (Lane) claims that musicians function as artists releasing their music in order to express an opinion they want the audience to hear. Yet he argues that the artist is only part of the equation, as, like other art, it must be interpreted; these interpretations may vary (2005). This equation is compounded when one considers corporate media's role in playing music. For Green Day, cutting through the incoherence became the theme and was the motivation behind their successful album which earned a Grammy Award for best album in 2005. The message behind *American Idiot* defies youth's passive acceptance of corporate media and challenges them to think for themselves.

There is undeniable success associated with initiating critical conversations induced by bringing popular culture through the music medium into the classroom since so many of the messages explored by contemporary artists are reflections of the larger society. These are not always popular messages, and inclusion within a curriculum is often criticized. However, Lisa DeLorenzo (2003) argues that music within the curriculum is one way to open up conversations about democracy when even choosing what to select within the curriculum and students' access to music is practice for critical debate.

Other critics argue that the messages in today's music actually create the problems in our society and should not be explored in any classroom settings. This may be illustrated in two ways. First, this problem is most significant to researchers interested in the hip-hop generation, which continues to practice misogyny toward black females (Roach 2004). Second, controversial legislation like the Patriot Act are prime discussion targets when artists like Steve Earle introduce political commentary like "The Revolution Starts Now."

Using lyrics as a text would diversify the curriculum and allow communication across various social groups (Houser 2005). According to Houser (2005), our role is both to promote and to involve students in civic affairs. This is not always achieved with curriculums that focus on standards-based instruction that does little to involve students, but it can be achieved using art and aesthetics "as a means of addressing these issues through citizenship education" (p. 45).

MUSIC FOR TEACHING AND LEARNING

Using music to enhance learning, to connect issues and the times in history, to illustrate a cultural identity, or to promote unity for a cause is not a foreign concept. While some realize the relevance behind the goals of making learning meaningful to students and, at the same time, illustrating a variety of major learning concepts to students, the task of moving beyond traditional learning styles to integrate other mediums is challenging and requires teacher flexibility and added research efforts. Is it worth the effort?

Popular Culture and the American Child (*Popular Culture and the American Child* 2000) claims that children spend approximately 10,500 hours listening to music. To highlight the significance of this number, consider that this is only five hundred hours fewer than they spend in school over their entire twelve-year enrollment. Surprisingly, over the course of students' years in school, the use of music in the classroom diminishes until it is almost nonexistent in the upper-level classrooms. This seems like an odd practice when so many junior high and high school students spend so much of their personal time listening to music. Silent support for this practice is demonstrated each time educators continue to keep the status quo with reliance on curricula that does not reflect the needs of the general student population, but rather policymakers' goals of standardization.

Studies show that American students do not recognize their role as active citizens as they credit societal changes to historical leaders rather than individual acts (Epstein and Shiller 2005). In other words, they do not believe that their voices are important. We must reverse this and prepare students to become critical, active citizens in a democratic society. A successful method to empower students early on is to show them that their point of views is valued and to accept their choices of media by allowing a variety of musical genres. All one need do is conduct an Internet search for musicians, songs, lyrics, or even connected themes in music such as protest songs, civil rights, or Civil War music, for example, to find an extensive list of possibilities. Educators may feel inhibited by the technological aspect of locating appropriate selections, but the actual task of acquiring this information is simple with MP3 technology and a computer as lyrics and individual songs are just a download away; students are happy to share their expertise in this matter. Considering how valuable the relatively recent explosion of music and other media available to educators, it is difficult to understand why that meaningful integration is still not employed.

Yet many in schools still seem threatened by the integration of music. What about specific school policy banning controversial materials such as contemporary music? What about possible complaints from parents and administrators? What about connecting the use of music to specific course objectives? Such questions are addressed with openness in one's teaching and learning. Periodic letters to parents outlining music integration ideas connected to course objectives help address concerns. Detailed lessons and units provided to administrators can also help. Classroom management techniques that focus on rights and responsibilities tied to integrating student choice in music also are integral to success. Perhaps even more important is the advocacy by teachers modeling and suggesting that integrating music facilitates lifelong skills development such as critical thinking and problem solving.

As suggested in the article, more emphasis should be placed on contemporary popular music in social studies. We promote a dual application of popular music. First, this allows educators to engage in powerful meaning making expeditions through a language that our students recognize and readily accept. Using this same language, we are then able to help students relate the meanings to a real-world context, both past and present. We would like to help students realize music's powerful effect on society and how it is often a collective call for civic action. Our ultimate goal is to use contemporary popular music as a enhancing social studies teaching and learning.

SAMPLE ACTIVITIES

When developing lessons centered on social studies themes like democracy and social justice, music is a powerful pedagogical method for examining songs from both the past and the present. To this end, Rosenthal (1998) offers a model which forces students to critically examine a variety of aspects including, (1) what is a social movement? (2) the exploration of the differentiation of pop and folk music; (3) the function of music for social movements; and (4) lyric exploration and to what extent they convey messages to the listeners. Here, the educator's role becomes more facilitating, encouraging students to make meaning of all materials presented.

Our first duty to students is to supply them with curricula that will be meaningful to them and that will help them be productive citizens in an ever changing society. This would be an impossible goal if students completed their requirements without helping to construct the content. Simply stated; the message in the music works and is powerful medium for engaging students in meaningful learning experiences.

MUSIC AND SOCIAL ISSUES

Introduction

Pass out lyrics to any song that deals with social issues such as "Where Is the Love," by the Blackeyed Peas.

Play the song, play other examples of songs that deal with social issues.

Ask the following:

What is the song about?

What issues and ideas are presented?

Why does the song begin and end when it does?

Place students in groups of approximately four.

Tell students that they are going to write their own lyrics on an agreed on social issue.

Have students individually brainstorm current social issues.

Have group members share.

Create a group stanza.

Pass out transparency and have groups write new stanza.

Each group will share and/or sing the new stanza.

Following the sharing have groups discuss rationale for events and/or issues included.

Groups

Individuals in groups brainstorm themes, social issues, and music examples for integration.

Brainstorm application ideas. Share.

Modeling

Have examples of music for groups to investigate.

Examples include songs from Public Enemy, System of a Down, Bob Dylan, Pete Seeger, Ani Defranco, Woody Guthrie, and so on.

Discuss the examples and choose specific examples of music for classroom integration.

Examples

Have lyrics and music for songs such as *Changes* by 2Pac, "Roll with It," by Ani Defranco, "Shimmy," by System of a Down

Groups should brainstorm integration ideas.

MUSIC AND TWENTIETH CENTURY

Introduction

Play two or three of your favorite songs (history, social themes). Inform students of the meanings, connections, and why you like the songs.
Have students do the following:
Write the names of three favorite songs.
Describe what the songs mean.
Why do you like the songs?
Bring in examples and/or lyrics.

Groups

Share examples. Have group members write or draw a response to the examples.
What are the similarities and differences between songs?

Discuss in groups

What are the elements of a good song or artist?
What kind of music do you like?
What are current issues regarding music in society?
What are your thoughts about these issues?

Extensions

Do the same with various themed collections such as:
Jukebox Hits of the 1950s, 1960s, 1970s, 1980s, and 1990s
Long Walk to Freedom
Say It Loud
Use various themes and/or issues in the music to teach or make connections to history and/or social issues.

Websites

Popular Songs in American History: www.contemplator.com/america
100 years of Music Posters: www.music-posters-history.com
This Day in Music History: http://datadragon.com/day
Black History in Music: www.rhino.com/blackhistory
Top 20 Music History: www.top20musichistory.com
Education Planet—History and Music: www.educationplanet.com/search/
search?keywords=history+and+music&startval2=0

Songs for Social Studies: http://songsforteaching.homestead.com/Social Studies.html

Teaching Media: www.media-awareness.ca/eng/med/class/teamedia/popcul.htm

Popular Culture Appreciation Society: http://home.vicnet.net.au/~popcult/net.htm#TOP

History in Song: www.fortunecity.com/tinpan/parton/2/history.html

CanTeach (Elementary Songs): www.canteach.ca/index.html

REFERENCES

Ali, L. (2002). Cries from the heart. *Newsweek*, October 28, 60–68.

Bafumo, M. (2004). Adding the arts. *Teaching Pre-K–8* 34(6): 8.

DeLorenzo, L. (2003). Teaching music as democratic practice. *Music Educator's Journal* 90(2): 35–40.

Epstein, T., and Shiller, J. (2005). Perspective matters: Social identity and the teaching and learning of national history. *Social Education* 69(4): 201–4.

Flaska, B. (2005). Odetta: Absolutely the best. www.popmatters.com/music/reviews/o/odetta-absolutely.shtml.

Harris, R. (2004). Middle schoolers and the blues. *Social Studies* 95(5): 197–200.

Hendrickson, M. (2005). Green Day and the palace of wisdom. *Rolling Stone*, 40–44. **[Au: Pls. supply day and month of publication.]**

Horn, R. 2003. Developing a critical awareness of the hidden curriculum through media literacy. *The clearing house* 76: 298–300.

Houser, N. (2005). Arts, aesthetics, and citizenship education: Democracy as experience in a postmodern world. *Theory and Research in Social Education* 33(1): 45–72.

Lane, J. (2005). Keep on rockin' in the free world: The advantages of using rock and roll in teaching social studies. w3.iac.net/~pfilio/lane.htm.

Palmer, J. (1998). Using songs as original sources in history and government. *The clearing house* 71: 221–223.

Popkin, H. A. S. (2005). Nothing shady about Eminem's new message, November 3. www.msnbc.msn.com/id/6362052.

Popular culture and the American child. (2005). www.mediascope.org/pubs/ibriefs/pcac.htm.

Rideout, V., Roberts, D., Foehr, U. (2005). Generation M: Media in the lives of 8–18 year-olds. *Executive Summary: A Kaiser Family Foundation Study*, March 2005. Henry Kaiser Family Foundation.

Roach, R. (2004). Decoding hip-hop's cultural impact. *Black Issues in Higher Education* 21(5): 30–32.

Rosenthal, R. (1998). Teaching a course on music and social movements. *Radical Teacher* 52: 15–20.

Roy, A. (2001). *Power politics*. Cambridge: South End.

Szatmary, D. (2002). *Rockin' in time: A social history of rock and roll*. Toronto: Prentice Hall.

13

Fight Club and the Disneyfication of Manhood

The topic of manhood fascinates me. When I was a young girl I was free to play within its borders, just as the younger boys did. When I was seven years old, my best friend, nine-hear-old James, saw no problem casting me as Napoleon Solo to his Illya Kuryakin in our *Man from U.N.C.L.E.* (1964–1968) reenactments. We played out our spy scenes quite happily until one day I found myself replaced by six-year-old Timmy. I did not understand at the time, but later I came to realize that James had become conscious of the fact that we were different, and with that consciousness came exclusion. Timmy replaced me in my role of Solo and I became the "girl." At that point I had no name or character identity beyond gender. I only played with them one or two more times after that. It was too boring.

"I AM JILL'S MISAPPROPRIATED MANHOOD"

Manhood confines man and masculinity, and ultimately exists to exclude, therefore creating the heterosexual dichotomy: us and them. Ultimately those who can somehow fit within the confines of manhood seem to gain an importance that we "others" do not. Butler (1990), writes that the unity of gender is the effect of a regulatory practice that seeks to render gender identity uniform through a compulsory heterosexuality (p. 31). The result is hypersexuality. Manhood becomes a parodic repetition, a Disneyfied or hyperreal version of itself, and our contemporary locus. This has led to a general sense of what Kimmel (1996) refers to as the "current male malaise" (p. ix). But how did we get here?

These days feminism and the woman's movement are fairly common-place in academic environments. This typically has not been true for stud-ies of manhood (Kimmel 1996). Interestingly, while a great deal of aca-demic attention has been focused on women's studies, theoretically helping girls better understand their world, until very recently little scholarship was available to help boys understand theirs. Just as feminist studies have added important information to the discourse, studies of manhood are of similar importance.

It may seem strange to consider the absence of studies of manhood since every text in our society seems to be centered in and reflective of male priv-ilege. It is often said that history is written by the winners, most often mean-ing Western European (white), wealthy, educated men. This helps explain why, until very recently, history textbooks contain so few stories of impor-tance about others in history. Authors of all textbooks, but especially those in history, have begun to include more inclusive perspectives on diverse people, places, and events across time. There has been a good deal of im-provement, however, the places at the table still are not as numerous or as valued: "if the book doesn't have the word *women* in the title, it's a good bet that the book is largely about men" (Kimmel 1996, 2). As efforts to im-prove the space for dialogic encounters continue for the others, the space for manhood seems to be fixed. Not only is the space for manhood rigid but the identifier is also set. As others have been claiming and defining space and appearing more prominently in the academic discourse, studies of manhood have been slower to evolve.

Kimmel (1996) points out that, despite the prominent focus on men, these texts do not explore the concept of manhood, or the experience of be-ing a man. Gender studies, he explains, are generally focused on women's experiences:

> We continue to treat our male military, political, scientific, or literary figures as if their gender, their masculinity, had nothing to do with their military ex-ploits, policy decisions, scientific experiments, or writing styles and subjects. As the Chinese proverb has it, the fish are the last to discover the ocean. (Kimmel 1996, 3)

Therefore, according to Kimmel, gender must become visible to men. His-tory must encompass the lives of both men and women, not just to include them merely because they are present as actors in an event. Gradually over time, feminist scholars have discovered the various meanings of woman-hood through history. Kimmel (1996) argues that manhood must undergo a similar process; scholars must begin to construct the meanings of man-hood across time.

These meanings are complicated by the media culture. Media supersatu-rates our world and influences our perceptions (Gitlin 2001). The conception of the real cannot be understood without an understanding that the real is no longer based on the real but rather on the media created real (Baudrillard 1994). Therefore in an investigation of manhood through history, it is impossible to extricate from a media influenced version of "real manhood." Therefore using a media text to examine the evolution of a media-ized version of manhood seems appropriate.

HISTORY CLASS TEXT

Most history teachers cover, in varying degrees of depth, the women's movements of the twentieth century in the United States. This does seem to tell an incomplete story. The history of manhood might be included in our classes to enrich our students' understandings of the people and events of the past, and the implications on their own present and future.

Baudrillard's (1994) theories of the simulacra may provide a useful frame to examine the evolution of these meanings of manhood through history. The three orders of the simulacra are:

- First order (the premodern period): The image is a clear copy of the real; the counterfeit.
- Second order (nineteenth century): Distinctions between image and representation begin to break down with mass production and the proliferation of copies.
- Third order (postmodern era): Representation precedes and determines the real; there is no longer any distinction between reality and representation, there is only the simulacrum.

When I began to think about where I could find a media representation of manhood, the movie *Fight Club* was in the top two (and I no longer remember the other possibility). This movie, *Fight Club* is manhood. It was an obvious conclusion, but as I watched it for the fifth or sixth time, I noticed that while manhood was at the center of the movie, it was not a constant; it seemed to float. While the filmmakers did not actually show the title of Baudrillard's (1994) seminal book (as they did in the movie *The Matrix* [1999]), it does seem fairly obvious that the "evolution" of manhood precedes through the stages of the simulacra from the real to the science fiction to the hyperreal. Students might develop a more powerful understanding of both Baudrillard's "precession through the simulacra" and manhood through an examination of the intersection of the two in the movie *Fight Club* (1999).

Media has often been used to teach history and historical concepts. Movies and television can be equally important teaching tools. Teachers who offer students the opportunity to examine the transformation of manhood across the simulacra go beyond traditional methods of merely teaching through popular media texts (for entertainment, relevancy, or the perceived immediacy of experience) and actually engage students to think critically about popular media texts.

THROUGH THE SIMULACRA . . . THE REAL

When the movie opens, the narrator (Edward Norton), in terms of manhood, is in the natural or real stage of the simulacra. In the beginning, manhood is warm and fuzzy. Our narrator acknowledges that he has become a duvet defining slave to the "Ikea nesting instinct" but seems happy to "flip through catalogs and wonder what kind of dining set defines me as a person." He says, "We used to read pornography now it was the Horchow collection."

But then things began to change for our hero. The yin and yang coffee table becomes an insufficient recipient of so much warmth and fuzziness. And our narrator stops sleeping. He explains to us that "with insomnia nothin's real, everything's far away, everything's a copy of a copy of a copy" (nearly as obvious a reference to Baudrillard as the one in *The Matrix*).

So the narrator begins the search for something more to care about. He discovers support groups including the "positive positivity" group. But he becomes most involved with the "Remaining Men Together" group, a support group for men with testicular cancer. There, as Cornelius (he had different names in each support group, which is a topic for another paper) he meets Bob. "Bob had bitch tits." Bob had been a "juicer," someone who used steroids to enhance his manly appearance. Ironically, his efforts to enhance his masculinity resulted in the removal of his testicles, a defining male appendage. Following his cancer diagnosis and surgery, the narrator explains, "subsequent hormone therapy made Bob develop bitch tits because his testosterone was too high and his body upped the estrogen."

Bob and the narrator are drawn together. Bob says "we're still men" to which the narrator replies, "yes we're still men, men is what we are." He goes on to explain "this was where I fit . . . between those huge sweating tits that hung enormous the way you'd think of god's as big." So our narrator realizes that he has become the "warm little center that the life of this world crowded around . . . Losing all hope was freedom." Every evening I died and every evening I was born again—resurrected.

In the "real" world, manhood was warm and fuzzy, caring about men who were not strictly defined as their physical characteristics, and could be easily understood through an examination of their home furnishings.

Then the character of Marla Singer is introduced to move the narrator into the next stage of the simulacra of manhood, the simulated real, or science fiction phase. Marla, the only female character in the movie, has a profound effect on the narrator. "Marla ruined everything . . . this chick . . . did not have testicular cancer—she was a liar. Marla, the big tourist . . . her lie reflected my lie . . . suddenly I felt nothing." And our narrator begins to suffer from insomnia again: "With insomnia you're never really asleep and you're never really awake."

"If I did have a tumor, I'd name it Marla. Marla the little scratch on the roof of your mouth that would heal if only you could stop tonguing it . . . but you can't."

The narrator offers to split up the support group sessions so that they could attend six each and on the seventh day they would alternate the "ascending bowel cancer" group. When he suggests to Marla that the testicular cancer group should be no contest, Marla explains that she has more of a right to be there than he has because he still has his balls. "On a long enough timeline the survival rate for everyone drops to zero."

ENTER THE PHYSICAL OF MANHOOD: TYLER DURDEN . . . THE SIMULATED REAL

Tyler splices single frames of male genitalia into family films such as *Cinderella*, urinates in the clam chowder at family restaurants, and knows that "one can make all kinds of explosives using simple household items."

Tyler appears just after the narrator loses everything, including a large portion of his dignity. The airline confiscates his luggage because it is vibrating, officials speculate about the source of the vibration: "9 times out of 10 its an electric razor but every once in a while, it's a dildo . . . of course it's company policy never to imply ownership in the event of a dildo . . . we have to use the indefinite article 'a' dildo never 'your' dildo." But when the suitcase was gone, "everything was gone . . . CK shirts and DKNY shoes."

And when his apartment blew up, everything else was gone. The other vestiges of his "real" manhood were destroyed. Although some comfort seemed to be found in that "losing all hope was freedom."

Over a beer, Tyler Durden comforts the narrator: "you know man, it could be worse . . . a woman could cut off your penis while you're sleeping and toss it out the window of a moving car." Tyler. Tyler is a survivor. Tyler wants to be in a fight because "how much can you know about yourself if you've never been in a fight. Who wants to die without any scars." It is the fights that ultimately sponsor the evolution of a critical mass of others into this second stage of the simulacra of manhood. Tyler's dream fight was with his dad: "My dad never went to college so it was real important that I go . . .

so I graduate and I call him up long distance . . . I say 'Dad, now what . . . he says 'get a job.' Now I'm 25, I make my yearly call and say 'Dad, now what?' He says, 'I don't know, get married.' We're a generation of men raised by women, I'm wondering if another woman is really the answer we need."

Through Fight Club, the men involved begin to see things differently. "I felt sorry for the guys packing into gyms trying to look like how Calvin Klein or Tommy Hilfiger said they should." When Tyler and the narrator were on the bus, they discuss a Gucci underwear ad that features a nearly naked male model. The narrator asks, "Is that what a man looks like?"

Apparently not in the second stage of the simulacra of manhood: the simulated real. There had to be scars: "Without pain, without sacrifice, we could have nothing."

Tyler Durden's long exchange with the narrator explains the manhood of the simulated real:

> This is the greatest moment of your life, man and you're off somewhere missing it. Shut up. Our fathers were our models for God. If our fathers bailed what does that tell you about God? Listen to me. You have to consider the possibility that God does not like you. He never wanted you. In `all probability he hates you. This is not the worst thing that can happen. We don't need him. F-- damnation, man. F-- redemption. We are God's unwanted children? So be it. [Narrator begs for vinegar to neutralize the burn of the lye Tyler had poured on his hand.] First you have to give up. First you have to know, not fear, know that someday you're gonna die . . . it's only after we've lost everything that we're free to do anything . . . [Tyler neutralizes the acid.] Congratulations, you're one step closer to hitting bottom.

ENTER THE DISNEYFIED MANHOOD:
TYLER *IS* JACK'S MANHOOD

Tyler Durden's second long exchange with the narrator foreshadows the move to the 3rd stage of the simulacra—the hyperreal.

> Man, I see in Fight Club the strongest and smartest men who've ever lived. I see all this potential and I see squandering. God damn it! An entire generation pumping gas, waiting tables, slaves with white collars. Advertising has its taste in cars and clothes. Working jobs we hate so we can buy shit we don't need. We're the middle children of history, man. No purpose or place. We have no great war, no great depression. Our great war's a spiritual war. Our great depression is our lives. We've all been raised on television to believe that one day we'd all be millionaires and movie gods and rock stars—but we won't. We're slowly learning that fact and we're very pissed off.

Tyler's soliloquies foreshadow the move to the next stage of the simulacra. He envisions a world where you are not your job. You're not how much money you have in the bank. You're not the car you drive. You're not the contents of your wallet. You're not your f-- khakis. You're the all-singing, all-dancing crap of the world. [Tyler as narrator] In the world I see you're stalking elk through the damp canyon forest around the ruins of Rockefeller Center. You'll wear leather clothes that will last you the rest of your life. You'll climb the vines that wrap the Sears Tower and when you look down you'll see the tiny figures pounding corn, laying strips of venison on the empty carpool lane of some abandoned superhighway.

The creation of Project Mayhem signals the beginning of the transition to the Disneyfied real. It is when Bob is shot that we realize that manhood has become hyperreal.

"His name is Robert Paulson." His name is Tyler Durden. Marla, the outsider, the woman, names him, defines him. Although his male alter ego must ultimately explain:

> You were looking for a way to change your life. You could not do this on your own. All the ways you wish you could be, that's me. I look like you wanna look, I f-- like you wanna f--, I am smart, capable, and most importantly, I am free in all the ways that you are not.

Project Mayhem will seemingly destroy all the vestiges of a simulated real manhood. By blowing up all the major financial institutions, manhood will again be defined by survival instincts. But the copy of the copy of the copy is still just a copy. Of course, that copy will be more real than the real. "Soap, the yardstick of civilization . . . Soap is made with lye and lye burns."

CONCLUSION

The curriculum of most schools emphasizes, at least rhetorically, students' critical thinking skill development. Movies can be important pedagogical tools to develop these skills. Further, in thinking about contextualizing, or understanding the history of manhood, Baudrillard's theories regarding the simulacra provide an important frame for thinking about the postindustrial world in which we live: the real, the simulated real, and the hyperreal.

RESOURCES

Baudrillard, J. (1999). *Simulacra and simulation.* Trans. S. Glaser. Ann Arbor: University of Michigan Press.

Butler, J. (1990). *Gender trouble: Feminism and the subversion of identity.* New York: Routledge.

Fight Club. (1999). Dir. D. Fincher. Twentieth Century Fox.

Foucault, M. (1990). *The history of sexuality.* Vol. 1. Trans. R. Hurley. New York: Vintage.

Fuss, D. (1989). *Essentially speaking: Feminism, nature, and difference.* New York: Routledge.

Gilman, S. (1986). Black bodies, white bodies: Toward an iconography of female sexuality in late nineteenth-century art, medicine, and literature. In H. Gates Jr., ed., *"Race," writing, and difference,* 223–61. Chicago: University of Chicago Press.

JanMohamed, A. (1986). The economy of Manichean allegory: The function of racial difference in colonialist literature. In H. Gates Jr., ed., *"Race," writing, and difference,* 78–106. Chicago: University of Chicago Press.

Palahniuk, C. (1996). *Fight club.* New York: Holt.

The Matrix. (1999). Prod. A. Wachowski and L. Wachowski. Village Roadshow Pictures.

14

Popular Culture and the Dark Side of Food

Food is a window into culture; it allows us to experience and sample cultures different from our own without leaving our homes; it serves as a means of transporting, transforming, and maintaining cultures. According to many, food is culture. Catherine Manton refers to food as everyone's first language (Manton 1999). Food can also be used as a tool to control or destroy culture. Food is necessary for all cultures to survive; to live, people must eat. But what of those who choose not to eat? Popular culture and food can, and have, become tools of self-destruction and frustration for many.

Food, consumerism, media, and the power of big business have a complicated and multifaceted relationship in American culture; separating them is difficult. Thin is the portrayed standard for beauty in this time and age and staying thin is a multi-million-dollar business. Images of thin, beautiful, and successful women are constantly bombarding us, implying that while being thin begets love and success, being fat, or even average to large, leads to one being unloved, unwanted, and unworthy. Yet food and the sharing of food is a basic part of who we are as a people.

We live in country that gives millions of dollars annually to combat hunger in developing countries. As of October 26, 2001, the United States had dropped 885,000 food rations into Afghanistan to keep the people from starving to death while dropping bombs to kill the Taliban soldiers. According to a story in the *Boston Herald*, when rumors of an antiterrorism bill that included embargos on food and medicine surfaced, the White House denied the report (2001). We do not want to be seen by the world as a country that withholds food from starving people. Indeed, it is considered politically incorrect to allow people to starve to death when we have

131

so much; to do so would betray our cultural image of being caring and humanitarian, even during a war.

The Food and Agriculture Organization of the United Nations defines food as a "fundamental right"(2001). People have a right to be free from hunger and a right to an adequate supply of food. Hunger causes hardships that directly impact global development. Hunger can lead to slowed mental performance and a loss of creativity; hunger can keep entire societies from reaching their full potential. The goal of the 1996 World Food Summit was to end hunger in our world. Oxfam America is dedicated to "creating lasting solutions to global poverty, hunger, and injustice"(2001). According to Oxfam statistics, the countries of the world produce enough food to feed everyone, yet 800 million people are hungry worldwide, and 31 million people are hungry in the United States. Education (or the lack of it), lack of resources and power, debt, trade, militarization and war, and discrimination are listed as the causes of hunger. The point that neither organization addresses is the many individuals in the United States and other developed countries who choose to be hungry. In a society filled with conspicuous consumption, where more is better, many are choosing to deny themselves food.

Defined as a potentially life-threatening neurotic condition, such as anorexia nervosa or bulimia, usually seen in young women, eating disorders affect approximately 8 million people in the United States today. Frances Berg, author of *Women Afraid to Eat*, and *Children and Teens Afraid to Eat*, speaks of a crisis in eating, and has identified six problem areas: dysfunctional eating, undernourishment of teenage girls, hazardous weight loss, eating disorders, size prejudice, and overweight (2001a, 18). In a society obsessed with image and weight, dysfunctional eating seems to have become the norm.

Many of us, children included, have chaotic eating patterns; we diet, miss meals, overeat, and binge. Popular culture, rather than discouraging dysfunctional eating, seems to inspire this behavior. We hurry from place to place, never far from our cell phones and pagers. Dieting is becoming a replacement for eating, with 50–80 percent of American women and girls on a diet at any given time (Berg 2001a). We eat to feel better when we are down, and we starve the next day to make up for it. Breakfast is frequently presented on television as a meal on the go. You can have your cereal and milk in a bar; you can pop a pastry in the toaster and carry it out the door with you. Dinner is frequently purchased through the drive-through window of a fast food establishment after sports activities and before dancing class. More and more families are two-income families, many with mom and dad both pursuing careers; as a result of our busy lives, we eat together as a family only 4.8 times a week on average (Berg 2001a). Nutritionists feel regular meals are essential to our well-being. Not only do regular meals tend to provide a more balanced and nutritious diet, eating together brings families together. When we share a meal, we tend to share our thoughts and feelings. Noted food writer M.F.K. Fisher was quoted as saying, "Sharing food with another human being is an intimate act that should not be indulged in lightly (Fisher 1949).

WOMEN AND FOOD

The relationship between women and food is as old as time itself, and just as complicated. Women have used food as a vehicle to nurture and care for others; they have used food as a symbol of friendship and love. Jewish and Italian mothers were stereotyped for years as always wanting, needing, to feed their family and friends. The more the family and friends ate, the happier the mother. Chicken soup became a prescription for physical and emotional ailments alike. Today, one very successful Italian restaurant chain advertises its food as being just like Mama used to make and Pillsbury sings, "Nothing says loving like something from the oven." If food and nurturing are bound together and women are the nurturers in our society, why have eating disorders become epidemic in our society?

Catherine Manton, author of *Fed Up* (1999), refers to food as a metaphor for the emotional lives of women, and she traces the beginnings of twentieth-century eating disorders in the United States to the Industrial Revolution and the rise of the food industry. The industrialization of food preparation removed the responsibility of caring and feeding the family from women and put it in the hands of "professionals," usually men. The H.J. Heinz family, owners of the Taggart Company (Wonder Bread), and many other entrepreneurs of the late nineteenth and early twentieth centuries, had to convince women that processed food was not only healthier for their families but brought rewards to the busy homemaker. Baby formula was developed and suddenly manufactured milk was healthier for babies than mother's milk. Women, who had been responsible for feeding their families and nursing their babies since time immemorial, were no longer up to the job. According to Manton, women became less confident in themselves and their self-esteem dropped because the traditional role of nurturer was taken away. It is estimated that eight million Americans have an eating disorder, and 90–95 percent of them are females. "To some degree, all women with eating disorders are unable to nurture themselves in ways that do not involve food or eating. A compulsive eater, for example is stereotyped as a nurturer who knows no boundaries. An anorexic woman cannot be nourished. A bulimic woman cannot sustain the nurturing process"(Manton 1999). Women have historically had a personal relationship with food; it has, until the twentieth century, been a positive relationship.

IMAGE, THE MEDIA, AND ADVERTISING

As the twentieth century progressed, the place of women in our society changed; 1920 brought the Nineteenth Amendment and women finally achieved suffrage. Until this time, beautiful women were not thin. During the Victorian Era, women were large and soft but had no political power or economic worth, other than that of their husbands. In fact, many considered thinness to be a sign of poverty or illness. The Nineteenth Amendment gave women political power, but it also coincided with the emergence of the Flapper and a thin body image. The Flapper style supposedly freed women from the conservative past, but in reality, the short hemlines and slinky dresses demanded that women be thin. The 1960s brought the next wave of the women's movement and once again, thin bodies were "in." Twiggy, at 5 feet 7 and ninety-one pounds, and designer Mary Quant set the standards for feminine beauty. As women demanded and received a better education and a place in the corporate world, the acceptable body size became even smaller, to the point of being unrealistic. Popular culture demanded that women show they were in control of their lives by being in control of their weight, the lower the better. Manton (1999) reports a study by Stewart (1996) that reported a $12,445 annual salary difference between overweight women and underweight women. The same study found that women at medically recommended weights also made less ($1,676 annually) than underweight women. "The message is clear-cut: women who are financially successful must have small bodies; education and ability are less important than physical appearance" (1999, 6). The only way for many women to have a small body is to deny themselves food and the pleasure that goes with enjoying food.

The role of the media cannot be overlooked or underestimated in the creation of the ideal female body. Popular television glorifies thin as sexy, successful, and happy. Such shows as *Sex in the City, Ally McBeal,* and *Friends,* not to mention the infamous *Bay Watch,* star thin women, specifically, young women with perfect bodies and faces who look great in small bathing suits. The power of television to transmit culture, and problems, is clearly demonstrated in Fiji. Television was introduced to this island nation in 1995, and there is only one channel. The impact nonetheless has been significant. Favorite programs include *Melrose Place* and *Xena: Warrior Princess.* In 1995 only 3 percent of the girls interviewed reported eating disorders; by 1998, 74 percent of the girls felt they were "too fat," and 62 percent said they had dieted in the past month; this is in a culture that has never held thin to be beautiful, but rather associates thinness with illness or poverty. One girl in the study expressed a desire to be like the "slim and very tall" girls on television. "We want our bodies to become like that . . . so we try to lose a lot of weight" (Chiu 2000).

Media influence goes far beyond television programs and magazines featuring glamorous women as role models. The media makes money by selling space, and advertising is a $130 billion dollar a year industry. Weight loss commercials make up 5 percent of television commercials today; prior to 1973, they did not exist. According to Berg, "advertising expertly conveys the message that you're not ok—and here's what you need to fix what's wrong" (Berg 2001b). Products are sold, along with body dissatisfaction, by perfect models. If we buy the products, we too will be perfect. Estee Lauder's spokeswoman, Elizabeth Hurley, exemplifies the idea of perfection; she is wealthy, successful, beautiful, and thin. Estee Lauder is a $3.6 billion corporation that controls 45 percent of the cosmetics market in the United States alone. *People* magazine published a study in 1996 that gave 5 feet 4 and 142 pounds as the average height and weight of American women, compared to 5 feet 9 and 110 pounds as average for the typical model (1996). The ideal woman is five inches taller and thirty-two pounds lighter than the real woman, and this so-called ideal size is not achievable for most of us, unless we don't eat. The *People* article also found 50 percent of the women interviewed were dissatisfied with way they looked.

Coca-Cola, an icon in the American marketplace, overstepped the bounds of politically correctness with an ad for Diet Sprite. Their model was a very thin young woman whose nickname was "Skeleton." In response to a public outcry, Coca-Cola pulled the ad. Calvin Klein is another well-known brand that uses very thin, young models. According to Berg (2001a), these types of advertisements send the wrong message about not only body size but also sexuality. Young consumers contribute a sizable amount of money to our economy, and corporations and advertising agencies recognize this. To make children the target of this type of advertising is morally wrong. It is ugly enough when it is directed at adults, but at least adults have the cognitive skills to recognize it for it is—an attempt to make money.

THE WEIGHT LOSS INDUSTRY

The weight loss industry, another power broker in the advertising and media game, arose in the 1950s and currently contributes between $30 and $50 billion annually to the U.S. economy. Catherine Manton attributes the growth of this industry to adversarial attitudes toward food consumption. As dieting has become more popular, the pressure to lose weight has increased for women in our society; 80 percent of the women in the United States diet regularly (Manton 1999). An industry that can not only reach but also convince 80 percent of the women in this country to dislike themselves enough to spend that much money is very powerful.

From its humble beginnings in Jean Nidetch's home in 1963, Weight Watchers has grown into a $418 million dollar business that made its debut on the New York Stock Exchange in November 2001 and boasts Sarah Ferguson, Duchess of York, as its spokesperson. The Weight Watchers connection to the food industry is interesting. It was purchased by the by H.J. Heinz Company, one of the best known corporate names in the United States, in 1978. Heinz sold all its interests, except the food products section, to Artal Luxembourg, and as of November 2001, Weight Watchers International is listed on the New York Stock Exchange.

I visited a Weight Watchers meeting and was told that this was a way of life based on healthy eating. The program requires a commitment; participants must pay a membership fee and weigh in on a weekly basis. The weekly meetings are support groups that offer positive reinforcement for pounds lost and encouragement to either keep losing or to maintain ideal weight, once it has been reached. Winning Points, their current program, assigns a point value to foods. Followers can eat anything they want, as long as they do not go over their daily allotment of points. A TV commercial featuring Sarah Ferguson said you could eat whatever you wanted, even chocolate cake, just as long as you stayed within your points. I can only imagine how many points a piece of chocolate cake, slathered with rich, fudge frosting, would be worth. Members are supported with pep talks and applause as they change their eating habits and reshape their bodies to be more like the perfect women seen on television and in fashion magazines. It also seems cultish; members belong and are supported in their efforts to become slender and remain that way.

Slim Fast, a popular food supplement that is available at neighborhood grocery stores, allows dieters to drink their meals. This idea takes away all of the social connections between people and meals. The corporate owners of Ben and Jerry's Ice Cream, and other brand names not known for low fat, Unilever, purchased Slim Fast in 2000. One has to wonder if the marketing strategy is to fatten us up, then slim us down, and make a profit doing both. Unilever is the third largest food corporation in the world. It also owns Bestfoods, which controls Hellmann's and Skippy peanut butter, neither of which is low in fat but does taste good.

The diet industry has not only brought us liquid meals and a point system that allows us to easily monitor our eating, it has also brought us fen-phen and other drugs to help us lose weight. Fen-phen, also known as a combination of the drugs fenfluramine and phentermine or dexfenfluramine, is currently the target of a class action lawsuit because it caused heart valve disease. Mass marketed under the name Redux, this drug combination was on the market from 1996 until the Federal Drug Administration pulled it off the market in 1997. Up to one-third of the people who took fen-phen may have damaged heart valves as a result. Primary pulmonary hypertension, a condition that can be fatal in four years, is also associated with fen-phen users. The Federal Drug Administration never approved the combination of these two drugs, and the only warning from that organization was that the drugs should not be used for more than one year. Berg states that fen-phen was only responsible for keeping ten or less pounds of the users (2001b). Damaged heart valves seem a rather high price to pay for the loss of ten pounds.

Many other weight loss drugs remain on the market and many are available without a prescription. They work by suppressing the appetite, speeding up the body's metabolism, blocking fat absorption, and, as a side effect, deadening the sense of taste. Phenylpropanolamine, PPA for short, is a common ingredient found in nonprescription, over-the-counter diet pills. The sale of these products is not regulated; teenagers can purchase them, and they are readily available at grocery stores, discount stores, and pharmacies. All of the boxes display a warning against use if you are pregnant or have high blood pressure. The warning labels also suggest that you discontinue using the products and consult your physician should you develop any side effects. They also should not be taken for indefinite periods of time, and when you stop taking them, they stop working. Berg reports that drug companies spend in excess of $40 million annually to market these products (2001b). If companies are willing to spend so much to market these over-the-counter weight loss drugs, the profit margin must be worth the expense.

CULTURAL ISSUES

Eating disorders were once thought to affect white, middle- and upper-class American women; recent studies, however, show this not to be true. The Something Fishy website on eating disorders reports that with the increase in the numbers of Hispanic and African American women competing in the professional job market, the numbers of minority women suffering from eating disorders has increased. They are faced with the mainstream image of the ideal woman–thin. To be successful, they must show that they are smart and in control of their lives and confirm to the ideal image.

The number of minority women in the media has also increased, and have become role models for minority females. Jennifer Lopez, Janet Jackson, Mariah Carey, and Gloria Estefan are all successful, glamorous, and thin. Oprah Winfrey, one of the most powerful women in the United States, has waged a war against her weight for years. Oprah has shared her ups and downs and her recipes with her fans, always trying to be thin. She is bright, articulate, loved and respected by millions, and still feels that she must diet. Her cook, Rosie Daley, published a cookbook of Oprah's favorite dishes. In the introduction of the book, Oprah wrote, "Some of my fondest early memories are of my grandmother over a stove fixin' food for our daily feast. I grew up eating well. . . . Food was the guest of honor, covering so much of the table there was hardly room for plates" (Daily1994, xi). Oprah also wrote that food meant comfort, security, and love.

While the numbers of minority women affected by eating disorders are rising, according to Berg, the numbers are still less than for white women (2001b). She reports that their idea of body image and beauty is much healthier than that of white females, and that they are accepting of many body sizes; they do not have to be thin to be beautiful.

As American culture spreads throughout the world, so do eating disorders. They seem to go hand and hand with increased consumerism and participation of women in the business and political spheres. Japanese psychologists are reporting eating disorders to be one of the most common health problems facing young women. Argentina, Sweden, Australia, Russia, Italy, and Great Britain are all seeing an increase in the number of women with anorexia or bulimia, and all are either industrialized countries, or in the case of Russia, a country on the fast track to a consumer-based economy. Great Britain is reporting 3.5 million anorexics or bulimics, with 6,000 new cases every year (Wolf 1991).

GIRLS, FOOD, AND SCHOOL

Puberty is a time of physical change that is often accompanied by feelings of inadequacy and confusion. Adolescents frequently become absorbed with how they look and how they think others perceive them; they tend to be very egocentric and feel their peers are constantly watching them. David Elkind refers to this self-absorption as adolescent egocentrism and identifies the imaginary audience as a facet of adolescent egocentrism (Parsons, Henson, Sardo-Brown 2001). Since adolescents tend view themselves as the center of their concern, they assume that others view them in the same light. This imaginary audience must be made to see them as perfect, and for many perfect is thin.

"Teenage girls have the poorest nutrition of any group in America. Taken as a whole, their diets are deficient in many important nutrients and in total calories"(Berg 2001a; 75). We are evidently feeding refugee groups more nutritiously than we are feeding our own daughters. A quick walk through the cafeteria of any high school or junior high would confirm this. I remember teaching eight graders who were dieting; lunch consisted of a diet drink. Young girls watch their mothers diet and assume dieting is the proper way to eat. They have been exposed to the ideal thin woman on television since they were toddlers.

Berg reports that 40 percent or more girls as young as fourth grade say they diet and that one-fourth of preteen white girls do not consume even half of the recommended 2,400 daily calories. Drawing from an unpublished study on calcium intake, Berg goes on to report that teenage girls are seriously deficient in calcium (2001; 80). The seriousness of the long-term effects of a calcium deficiency are staggering, especially when you stop to consider that we spend millions trying to prevent just this type of problem in developing countries. Iron and zinc deficiencies are common in teenage girls. Berg sites a British study that reported a drop in iron levels caused a significant drop in IQ scores (2001a); the implications of this on our society are frightening. Iron deficiency leads to anemia, which leads to fatigue and a shortened attention span. Children who do not eat meat are the most at risk for developing an iron deficiency, and meat is one of the first foods girls stop eating. Meat is also a main source of protein, which is necessary for healthy bodies and minds.

If girls come to school hungry, they will not develop to their full potential. When you are hungry, your powers of concentration are not sharp; your attention span is short. Your mind cannot learn if your stomach is empty. We serve free and reduced-price breakfast and lunch to children from low-income families to improve their learning, but we ignore girls who are starving themselves to be fashionable.

The image of thin as beautiful is alive and well in most of our high schools. As a general rule, large girls are excluded from drill teams and cheerleading squads. Drill teams, dance groups, and cheerleaders do not, as a rule, have heavy girls performing if they do make the team for political reasons. One 5-A high school in an upper-middle-class community in Texas prides itself on its drill team, among other things. At one point the senior officers were weighing the underclassmen on weekly basis; "overweight" girls were not allowed to perform during halftime. Out of thirteen freshmen girls on the team, several were reported to be bulimic. The sponsor, a coach, looked the other way. The costumes and uniforms are frequently skimpy and tight fitting and are not becoming on large bodies. The high school mentioned above used the junior high feeder school as a training ground for future members. Thirteen- and fourteen-year-old girls were being told to lose weight so they would look good in their dance costumes.

The problem with not being a thin student does not end with the drill team. Overweight children are frequently the target of teasing and ridicule by other students. I have heard teachers speak negatively about large children, especially girls, referring to them as lazy and stupid. Physical education class can be particularly painful for them; they are often forced to dress out and reveal their not so small bodies to a critical audience. Coaches have been known to single "fat kids" out for attention and extra laps. These children frequently stay on the sidelines of school life, hoping no one will notice that they do not measure up to the ideal look. Many overweight, or just large, teenagers develop a low self-esteem that carries over into adulthood. Worse, many of them stop eating to achieve the look of perfection.

WHAT SCHOOLS CAN DO

Schools should be a place of safety and acceptance for children of all sizes. We need to provide role models other than fashion models and entertainment idols for young girls. A curriculum that looks at the contributions of women in general, the Eleanor Roosevelts and Helen Kellers of the world, not just the Pamela Andersons, would be very beneficial here. Young girls need to see women who do not have perfect, thin bodies in successful and influential positions.

Schools need to stress health, especially in middle and high school. Health is required in many states, Texas for one, and is frequently considered a "blow off" course. Healthy eating habits and nutrition should be presented along with facts about eating disorders. School food service departments need to plan and offer food that tastes good and market it in such a way to make students want to eat it.

Vending machines, a source of funds for schools, need to be regulated. Available before school, during lunch, and just about any other time, they provide a diet drink for breakfast and lunch. For many girls, this is the only lunch they choose to have; it is fat free. Since 1987, soft drink consumption as tripled (Berg 2001a). Soft drinks are actually promoted because the school receives a portion of the proceeds from the vending machines; they do not receive any of the proceeds from milk.

Counselors and teachers, especially coaches, need to be educated about eating disorders and trained to recognize the symptoms. Coaches are in a unique position because they see children in a slightly different environment than the regular classroom teacher. Instead of weighing students in, they could concentrate on helping all children feel comfortable in their bodies by stressing health. Counselors need to have the time to work with students who have problems. Support groups are one method currently being used in many schools to offer support and education to girls suffering from eating disorders. Obviously the students they serve must view the schools as a place of safety and sanctuary, or the programs will not work. Prevention needs to be the focus, not curing, if we want to control the damage wrought by eating disorders.

CONCLUSION

For many years, eating disorders were considered to be the disease of white middle- and upper-class American women. A 1984 publication by the ERIC Clearinghouse on Counseling and Personnel Services described bulimia and anorexia as binge eating and starving disorders that affected thousands of middle-class white teenage girls and young women each year (Hebert

1984). Today we are seeing eating disorders in females of all ethnic groups and developing countries.

The popular cultural infatuation with perfection and beauty must be changed if we are to cure our society of this problem. If the media chooses to bombard us with images of thin women, we must stop buying into the image. Our culture needs to become more focused on what we do as people, rather than how we look. We must return to the traditional relationship between women and food, one of harmony and enjoyment. Food needs to be returned to its place as a tool to nurture us and provide social interaction. We need to enjoy food and eating.

REFERENCES

Berg, F. (2001a). *Children and teens afraid to eat.* 3rd ed. Hettinger, ND: Healthy Weight Network.

———. (2001b). *Women afraid to eat.* Hettinger, ND: Healthy Weight Network.

"Bush said to be seeking new food embargo power." (2001). http://bostonherald .com/cgi-bin/epr.../ausembar0929001.htm.

Chiu, A. (2000). TV trouble in paradise: The small screen brings eating disorders to Fiji. www.abcnews.go.com/sections/liv...eatingdisorders_990519.htm.

Cultural roles. (2004). www.something-fishy.org/cultural/roles.php.

Daley, R. (1994). *In the kitchen with Rosie.* New York: Knopf.

Fisher, M. F. K. (1949). *The Columbia world of quotations.* www.bartleby.com/66/2/ 22202.html.

Food and Agriculture Organization of the United Nations. (2001). Food: A fundamental human right. www.fao.org/Focus/E/rightfood/right1.htm.

Hebert, D. (1984). Eating disorders: Counseling issues. www.ed.gov/databases/ ERIC_Digests/ed260367.html.

Manton, C. (1999). *Fed up women and food in America.* Westport, CT: Bergin & Garvey.

Oxfam America. (2001). In a world of abundance, why hunger? www.oxfamamerica .org/fast/text_activities.html.

Parsons, R., Hinson, S., Sardo-Brown, D. (2001). *Educational psychology a practitioner-researcher model of teaching.* Stamford, CT: Wadsworth.

Too fat? too thin? (1996). *People,* June 3, 64–74.

Wolf, N. (1991). *The beauty myth.* New York: Doubleday.

15

Toys, Play, and Learning

As my eyes scan the room, I see several groups of excited five- and six-year-olds playing with various toys. I wonder to myself if these are the kind of toys the children have in their home. I begin to observe one group building a farm with blocks of various sizes and shapes. As the building begins to take form, the children add various animals and begin to decide which animal should go in which part of the farm. Another group is constructing cars and trucks with Legos. Some children are making cookies with play dough and a group of children are in the home center cooking using various dishes, pots, and plastic food items. As I walk around the room, I take in all the conversation going on between various children and realize that what I have been learning about play is actually taking place.

The children are playing in their own environment with different toys. At the same time, though, there is learning going on. As I watch the children building the farm, I hear them talking about which blocks to use. I hear one tell another that a particular block would be better for building the fence for the horses. I realize that various strategies of learning are being used. I hear various types of math strategies, classification, measurement, as well as building new vocabulary as the children talk to each other. As I watch and listen to the children with the Legos, I see them experimenting with different types of wheels for their cars and trucks. When I ask why they are using a certain kind, their response is that the wheel they have chosen will make the car go faster. In the home center, I see lots of interaction going on as the children prepare a meal. They decide how to set the table, which pot to cook in, which things are for cooking, and where everyone is to sit at the table. It is interesting to me that children can create and imagine almost anything as I'm sure they have been doing since time began. It is also interesting to me which toys they choose to play with.

Toys are the tools of children's play. Toys influence play. Toys of value enhance children's own ideas. They help the child to engage in imaginative, meaningful play by allowing them to solve the problems. Sometimes the toys they choose are ones they are already familiar with or have played with before. Other times a toy is chosen because it is new and presents lots of challenges. Often one child will choose a toy and another will want to play with it when maybe they have never played with that particular toy before.

I wonder if popular culture is influencing this kindergarten classroom even without the media influence that so many children receive when they go home. I decided to survey of the children to find out what their favorite toys at home were and found out that most of them picked toys they have seen on television but we do not have in the classroom. Only a couple of children even had blocks at home. Several of them had Legos and lots of the girls had dishes and plastic food. Some of the boys with sisters also had that. It became interesting to me how toys are often in categorized according to gender.

I observed a toy store to see how toys are placed on the shelves and which children were visiting which shelves. The cars and trucks are together and are often visited by boys, whereas the baby dolls and Barbies are together and those isles had only girls in them. It was also interesting to me that when you enter the store there was a large stuffed animal that is featured in the latest children's movie. As we know, advertising is at an all-time high when it comes to children's toys and it peaks at holiday time. The electronic games and equipment are grouped together and it was interesting to see children of all ages and genders in those isles, including many adults. This is what led me to decide to study the history of toys and how toys affect children's play. Play is very important in early childhood education because children learn so much while play is taking place. Developmental psychologists since Jean Piaget have maintained that infants and young children learn new concepts through a dual process: first discover and then practice.

HISTORY OF TOYS

Toys have been around forever. Children of the first humans played in much the same way and for the same reasons that young animals play. They often played by copying their mother's movements. It helped them to learn behavior and survival. Sumerian princes played board games about 4,500 years ago. As each new age developed, new and different toys emerged. Romans loved board games and played a favorite known as three stones, which was a bit like tic-tac-toe of today.

During the Middle Ages, children learned games such as chess, backgammon, and board games that were centered on battles. When the Europeans crossed the Atlantic in the 1500s, they brought dolls, which are believed to be among the first items to be traded with the Indians. Soon dolls were made everywhere and sold by traveling peddlers. It was during the 1800s that inexpensive toys began to be made. By the 1880s, factories in the United States were supplying the world with large numbers of toys.

By the 1900s great changes were taking place and children were fascinated with cars, trucks, airplanes, and ships. It was in 1903 that a new toy appeared on the store shelves—the teddy bear. All sorts of stuffed animals could be seen in stores alongside the teddy bears. In 1928 a famous name was born when Walt Disney created Mickey Mouse. Today the character is closely related in films and television programs for children.

In the 1970s and 1980s, there were all kinds of developments in the world of toys. The first video game was invented in the United States in 1972. Personal computers became common in every home by the 1980s. Many were based on board games, while others were fantasy adventures. Electronic games were moving into a new realm with voice commands and headsets that create a "virtual reality" world. Children play games on the Internet, which allows players to communicate at a high level of interactivity. This is all exciting as our world keeps changing and inventions go to a higher and higher level. But we shouldn't forget that the human brain is more incredible than any computer. Even small children have the power to imagine and make believe. They have been doing that for thousands of years.

PLAY AND THE MEDIA

"Play is foundational to creativity in children and adults because it is our playfulness that links the child within each of us to the child we teach." (Isenberg and Jalango 1997). Most early childhood experts believe that play is important to learning. It enables children to make sense of their world, develops social and cultural understandings, provides opportunities to meet and solve problems, fosters flexible and divergent thinking, allows children to express their thoughts and feelings, develops language and literacy, and develops concepts in all academic areas. It is through play that toys and games are incorporated.

Since the 1950s, corporations have been producing more and more of our children's experiences. Video games, TV, movies, and music are now a private domain of children. Traditional notions of childhood as a time of innocence and adult dependency have been undermined by children's access to popular culture during the twentieth century. Many of the toys on the market today are highly structured and linked to TV and videos. These toys channel children into imitative play, robbing them of their own imagination, problem solving, and creativity.

As teachers we must ask ourselves if the children who are spending all the time in this popular culture are truly thinking for themselves or is the culture thinking for them. Children average thirty-five hours per week in front of a screen either watching TV and videos or playing video games (Postman 2005). Are they able to distinguish real from make-believe? Do they create things of their own design and thoughts? Are they eager to share ideas with those around them or have they become used to being isolated? These are things we need to consider when we teach young children.

Many of the messages in the media can undermine their sense of safety and trust. There needs to be the freedom in the classroom to discuss what children see on TV, what music they listen to, and what games they play. But at the same time children need to be given opportunities to explore, create, experiment, internalize, socialize, and learn in an environment that is not always controlled by school institution rules, but also is not totally left to rely on what they see and hear in media.

Trying to ban media-influenced play from the classroom is often unsuccessful. It denies children the opportunity to understand what they see in the media (Daspit and Waever 2000). Observing children and their actions can help you understand how they interpret what they see. Early childhood teachers are often confronted with children asking if something or someone is real that they have seen on TV. They have a hard time believing what I tell them because they are young and innocent and feel what the TV says is true. We, as educators, must understand and be aware of what children are exposed to in order to understand what they are referring to and being able to help them understand the real from the fantasy.

Marketing products to children has reached a new high since video games have expanded to trading, playing, and collecting the cards; successful films which skyrocket in revenues; and T-shirts and other children's merchandise peddled by a variety of stores. These are all pitched to the nation's youngest consumers, even kindergartners, who now command millions in sales through the effort of parents to please their kids. Keeping up with the latest version costs lots of money. Often parents buy whatever is the popular item without investigating the effect it will have on their child. They often don't even pay attention to the safety features or the age appropriateness. Teachers have reported that recess, once a time when children would run around, play sports, and let off steam, is being transformed into trading sessions of collectible cards and other toys. "Learning to share" doesn't work very well in the competitive world of toy paraphernalia.

Children in the United States are born into a consumer-driven society. Starting at birth, relatives and friends give children toys or objects to express love. The child develops a sense of well-being. The world outside the family plays an important role in a child's life. Media shapes ideas and standards which children uncritically accept. Toy manufacturers spend millions of dollars advertising to children about toys. Trends and fashions in youth culture are not a new phenomenon. When children get attached to a certain style of dress or a certain type of toy or music, it often defines that generation, such as the Mods or Rockers of the 1960s, the punk era of the 1980s or hip-hop of today. The difference is that there is an increase today in the availability of consumer goods and the use of the media to promote these goods.

The pressure to adopt a certain lifestyle or a certain toy product starts early. By the age of eighteen, the average child in the United States will have seen between 350,000 and 640,000 commercials on TV (Giroux 2001). Sometimes it only takes one viewing for a child to feel he has to have that particular toy. Some children feel they have to have a particular toy to be happy. Some children feel they have to have a certain toy in order to play. In the past, children would grab whatever they could find to play. Now they are being told that in order to play you need a particular toy. It has built a dependence on objects for play and undermined children's basic sense of self-sufficiency in play.

In 1959, the United Nations adopted the Rights of the Child, which included a "full opportunity to play" as one basic right of childhood (Carlsson-Paige and Levin 1990). This means providing basic economic and social supports, which are prerequisites for healthy play. It means providing an environment in which children have the freedom to construct their own dramas built out of their own interpretations of reality. Most children in the United States are not ensured of that and we are a long way from providing it for them. This would mean some extreme changes in the world of toy manufacturing. We need to understand the way children think and learn, and what their needs are, and put aside our adult ideas and just think about what is best for children. "Experts have voiced concern that the push to stress academics in earlier grades leaves little room for emotional and social development" (Education Week 2000). This is a danger that will greatly affect our children.

CONCLUSION

It is interesting which toys become a child's favorite and which toys last as best-sellers. As I surveyed children and adults, I experienced different thoughts and feelings when a particular toy was classified as the favorite. Sometimes a toy was a favorite because someone special gave it to the person. Sometimes the toy was the favorite because it was fun to play with.

Sometimes the toy was ranked as favorite because the person had fond memories playing with the toy and a favorite person. For whatever reason, toys stay around because they bring pleasure and joy to a person. When interviewing adults, big smiles crossed their faces when asked what their favorite toy at the age of six was and why it was their favorite. But children had those same smiles on their faces when asked the same question even though their toys had not been around on their shelves or in the closets for as long as the adults. One thing for sure, toys are endearing for the fun had when playing, the fun had when learning, and the security gained when the toy was near.

If we as parents and educators remember and understand the importance of play in a child's life and use that in the selection of toys, we will get back to the basics of preparing children to become adults. The words of the ancient Chinese proverb, " I hear and I forget. I see and I remember. I do and I understand," will take on a whole new meaning with our children. Toys will be around as long as there are children. Toy manufacturers will constantly be changing the toy world in order to make money. Toy stores will stock toys for children based on the latest movies and fads, but in reality it is sort of a dual process that depends on each part.

Children pick and buy toys based on the media, yet the manufacturers create the toys based on what they think the children will buy. Children will select toys on the basis of enjoyment and challenge. Children will continually select and manipulate materials in the environment to keep up interest. In other words, to stay stimulated children will continue to choose and buy new toys. Popular culture does influence what kind of toys will be on the shelves each Christmas holiday, but a child's choice will decide the longevity and the endearing factor. Endearing is a word that means "expressing affection or well liked." Popular means "liked by most people or by many" (*Webster's* 1994). A toy may be popular at the time it is purchased, but how long will it stay that way? The very next year you may see a totally different line of toys on the shelves of toy stores.

Children will play with lots of different toys for lots of different reasons, but when choosing their favorite, that is different entirely. They choose a toy as their favorite for the meaning attached to it, whether that is the fact it has lasted the longest or whether someone special gave it to them. If we were to take a journey into many attics and find the boxes marked as keepsakes, it would be interesting to see which toys would be there and why. As the old song says, "Everything old is new again." That is true of toys. If we were to bring those boxes down from the attic and peek inside with the owner, we would begin to see smiles and hear stories of days when that particular toy was received, when it was played with, and who was around when the playing was taking place. That is the endearing factor of a toy, not what is popular on the shelf.

As I scan the children in my classroom again, I begin to notice that the toys in my classroom have endearing qualities and some have popularity among the students. Some of the toys that are returned to for playing seem to be favorites because the child can change them in some way. Some of the toys present a new challenge to the child. I sometimes put some toys away for a period of time so I can encourage children to play with other things in the classroom. Then later I will bring that toy back to the shelf and a new awareness of discovery takes place. I always find it fascinating to watch which children choose which toys. I know one thing for certain—children love to play and they love to play with toys. I also know from watching children at play that one toy can be created into lots of different things according to the child's imagination. We celebrate the children's birthdays during the year. Many of the toys on their list are things seen on TV or in a magazine that advertises the "latest and greatest" toys. I wonder what a child would do if that particular toy was not given and another toy with creative potential in learning were placed under the tree instead. I know there would be disappointment, but would play begin?

REFERENCES

Alverman, D., Moon, J., Hagood, M. (1999). *Popular culture in the classroom.* Newark, DE: IRA.
Carlsson-Paige, N., and Levin, D. (1990). *Who's calling the shots?* Philadelphia: New Society.
Daspit, T., and Weaver, J. (2000). *Popular culture and critical pedagogy.* New York: Taylor & Francis.
Education Week. (2000). April 12.
Education Week. (2000). February 16.
Education Week. (2000). January 12.
Education Week. (2000). December 6.
Giroux, H. (2001). *Stealing innocence.* New York: Palgrave.
Isenberg, J., and Jalongo, M. (1997). *Creative expression and play in early childhood.* New Jersey: Prentice Hal.
Postman, N. (2005). *Amusing ourselves to death.* New York: Penguin.
Steinberg, S., and Kincheloe, J. (1997). *Kinderculture.* Boulder: Westview.
Steele, P. (1999). *Toys and games.* Watt, Franklin.
Webster's new world dictionary. (1994). New York: Prentice Hall.
Wulffson, D., and Keller, L. (2000). *Toys!* New York: Holt.

WEBSITES

www.lionlamb.org/Top_20_2000-2001.html
www.discovery.com/stories/history/toys/otherlist.html

www.yesterdayland.com/popopedia/shows/categories/toys
www.aap.org/family/mediaimpact.htm
www.childcareaware.org/en/dailyparent/0199/
www.truceteachers.org
www.theonion.com/onion3639/montessori_school.html
www.nncc.org/Curriculum/create.play.grow.html
www.intac.com/~slalbert/redirct2.html
www.btha.co.uk/publications/ntc/toytrends.html

16

Reading Printed Pop Fiction

Graphic Novels in the Classroom

These days if you ask a youngster between eleven and fifteen what his of her favorite book is, chances are it will be a graphic novel. The popularity of graphic novels has increased dramatically in recent years, making it the fastest-growing segment of the publishing industry, growing from $75 million in 2001 to $120 million in 2004 (Publishers Weekly, 2007).

If graphic novels are new to you, here is a list of basic vocabulary:

- Comics: A collection of pictures and words that together tell a story. Historically rooted in the funny papers of the early twentieth century. Often superhero themed and serialized.
- Graphic novels: A collection of pictures and words that together tell a story. Term was coined to distinguish these works from other funnies or children's comic books. They are, for the most part, self-contained rather than serialized, and are longer than comics. More complex than comics and address themes and conflicts usually found in more traditionally accepted forms of literature.
- Anime: Japanese animation (on film).
- Manga: Japanese term, roughly translated means "comic" (in print).
- Shounen/shonen: Subgenre of manga marketed to male readers up to the age of eighteen.
- Shoujo/shojo: Subgenre of manga targeted to female readers up to the age of eighteen.

Publishers in the United States since the 1950s have marketed comics, typically based around superhero themes, primarily to boys. Whether this was the cause or effect of low readership among girls is unknown. In Japan, comics, called manga, cover a wide range of genres and are marketed successfully to groups of all ages, both boys and girls. In the late 1990s as manga caught fire in the United States, publishers were caught unprepared and are still trying to catch up with the demand for shoujo manga. Publishers and producers of manga in the United States, mostly males, wrongly assumed that girls would be looking for romance comics or soap opera digests. The difference between comics produced in the United States and the most popular shoujo from Japan is the degree to which they focus on human interaction. Over the past thirty years in Japan the mainly female producers of shoujo have searched for the most intuitive ways to depict conversation, emotional states, and human nature in graphic form. Based on their popularity, they have obviously been successful in developing a visual language sufficient to reach these lofty goals.

RATIONALE FOR CLASSROOM USE

The mandate for reading instruction and/or practice permeates the current public school curriculum. This, combined with our increasingly visual culture, suggests that students will benefit greatly from the use of graphic novels in the classroom. Teachers should not worry that graphic novels "dumb down" or discourage reading more traditional texts. Lavin (1998) suggests that reading text and images together requires more complex cognitive skills than reading text alone. When words vanish altogether, the skills required to decode the visual messages in the panels are certainly at a higher cognitive level.

In the social studies, especially history, textbooks are typically generic, boring, and bland (Kincheloe 2001; Loewen 1995). Graphic novels on the other hand are produced by a diverse group of authors and present views of culture, history, and human life in accessible ways. These novels allow students to examine content and concepts in new and different ways, and the visuals help them develop skills and strategies to imagine history.

Graphic novels are just like anything new you try in the classroom. Both teachers and students will need time and patience. Many students, because they read them for fun, might consider themselves experts on reading these books, although they may need to be pushed a little to begin to critically consider their content. For students who are less familiar with the graphic text format, it will be important to provide basic reading instruction.

READING GRAPHIC NOVELS: BEGINNERS

Graphic novels interweave images and text which must be read together. Reading images involves several steps. The first step for readers is to notice what is most noticeable, that is, identify and consider the first thing to strike their eye. Readers should then begin to consider the people, objects, and activities portrayed in the image. How are these elements arranged? Who are the people in the image? What do they look like, including their expressions, and what are they doing? Where are they—what is the setting? What objects are visible, including those in the background? Readers should consider all the things they see in the image, and they should also consider what is not seen. This is sometimes more important to the story than what can be seen in the actual image.

Once the image has been analyzed, Gravett (2005) recommends reentering the panel and moving your eyes around to scan all text, noticing whether it is a comment (box), a speech (balloon), or thought (cloud). The actual text reveals much about what is being said and who is speaking. There are many ways that emotion can be indicated—literally through the actual word or through type formatting, if the text is in bold or all capital letters. The text balloons can also reveal emotion. For example, text in a balloon with jagged edges probably indicates an extreme emotion. A wavering border on a text balloon might indicate a speaker's exhaustion.

Each panel on a page must be considered individually as well as collectively. Panels should be read from top left to bottom right, unless it is in the Japanese style (manga) from right to left.

STANDARDS AND SELECTIONS

There are an increasing number of graphic novels being published, and many of them would be good choices for a history classroom. Novels might be chosen based on content, or on a particular historical concept or theme. They might also be chosen to develop a particular skill. The Office of the Superintendent of Public Instruction (OSPI) in Washington State has identified inquiry, interpersonal, and critical thinking skills as most necessary for encouraging responsible citizenship among students. According to its website, OSPI defines a responsible citizen as one who "uses a wide range of social studies skills, including critical thinking, to investigate and analyze a variety of resources and issues and seek answers" (www.k12.wa.us/ curriculumInstruct/SocStudies). Social studies skill development is related to every grade level.

In addition to providing scaffolded skill development, Washington State social studies instruction in the primary grades should consist of integrated themes that will provide context/schema for more specific content learning in later grades. The themes for primary grades include:

• Individual development and identity: Learning about myself, classroom community, and the food we eat

- Families: In our community and in other places
- Our community: How they meet our needs and wants
- People, places, and environments: Cultures in our community, our Native American past, and making global connections

Even in the more specific instructional standards for the higher grades, students must grasp certain concepts before historical events can truly be understood. In the intermediate grades, the study of Washington State and United States history requires several prerequisite concepts, especially responsible citizenship. If that concept development began in the primary grades, teachers at the intermediate level might ask students to consider: *What does good citizenship mean? What do communities require citizens to do and understand?* Once they understand the general concept of responsible citizenship, students may then utilize that knowledge as a frame in which to examine the unique history, geography, and governmental structure of Washington State.

The concept of civic ideals and practices is also necessary to understand the history of the United States. Colonization, independence, and events up through the present day can only be fully understood if we frame that knowledge in an understanding of what we as citizens in a democratic society aspire to and how those aspirations manifest in reality.

Graphic novels will provide opportunities for skill and concept development for students at all levels. An example for primary grades might be *Monkey vs. Robot* (2000) by James Kochalka. According to the book's summary, it is "an exciting action-packed rumble-in-the-jungle! A factory of self-replicating robots is stripping the jungle of its natural resources, threatening the territory of a colony of nearby monkeys. A series of encounters between the two groups quickly escalates into all out war." This book could be used with younger students to teach the concepts of community and of needs versus wants. Because the graphic novel is not overt in its approach to teaching this concept, students must apply their inquiry skills to make the necessary connections. The use of this novel would provide a means for creating conceptual understanding as well as an opportunity for important skill development.

An example of a graphic novel that might be used in the intermediate and middle school grades is *Alia's Mission: Saving the Books of Iraq* (2004) by Mark Stamaty. The author recounts the heroic story of Iraqi librarian Alia Muhammad Baker as she rescues over 30,000 volumes from her library in Basra before it's besieged. One reviewer on Amazon.com writes that the book is "a fast-paced and informative Middle Eastern study for younger audiences." This book offers the reader both conceptual and factual learning opportunities. Concepts include most all those emphasized in the social studies in the early grades: individual development and identity, community, and people, places, and environments. Inquiry skills might be applied to focus on the following ideas: that ordinary people can become heroes in extraordinary circumstances; communities must document their achievements and must preserve and safeguard those artifacts for their future generations; all societies in the world have unique and important histories. Students may use this book to gain factual knowledge about Iraq, its history, geography, and present-day issues. The book also offers information for students to be able to place Iraq in the larger context of the Middle East region. This would be particularly relevant to sixth grade teachers in Washington State as they begin to meet the world geography and world history standards specified in the social studies curriculum.

Students must begin concept and skill development in the early grades so that teachers at the secondary level can make connections to that schema. It is only through these connections, as well as the ensuing historical literacy, that students can approach a more accurate historical understanding of a historical period, person, place, or event. As in the earlier grades, graphic novels for secondary students might emphasize concept development or communicate some factual information. A novel such as *Barefoot Gen* (2004) by Keiji Nakazawa offers students a unique look at the experiences of an ordinary Japanese family who opposed Japanese involvement in World War II, the persecution that the family suffered because of this stance, and also the experiences of some citizens of Hiroshima in the aftermath of the atomic bomb dropped by the United States. In addition to new content knowledge, *Barefoot Gen* offers students the opportunity to strengthen their conceptual understandings of responsible citizenship, including rights and responsibilities in a democracy compared to other types of government.

These are only three examples of a growing number of graphic novels that are available and suitable for classroom use. There is a large number of titles that can be used with students at almost all reading levels and grade levels. Teachers at the lower grade levels have an important responsibility to introduce students to the important concepts of history. Washington State has established a set of essential academic learning requirements (EALR) for social studies content knowledge (history, geography, economics, and civics) and skills at every grade level. Teachers must decide the best way for their particular students to meet those learning objectives. There are many reasons why graphic novels are an important teaching and learning tool, including the availability of a wide range of titles and the popularity of this type of text among young people.

REFERENCES

Gravett, P. (2005). *Graphic novels: Stories to change your life*. London: Aurum.
Kincheloe, J. (2001). *Getting beyond the facts: Teaching social studies/social sciences in the twenty-first century*. New York: Lang.

Kochalka, J. (2000). *Monkey vs. robot.* Marietta, GA: Top Shelf Productions.

Lavin, M. (1998). Comic books and graphic novels for libraries: What to buy. *Serials Review* 24(2).

Loewen, J. (1995). *Lies my teacher told me: Everything your American history textbook got wrong.* New York: New Press.

Nakazawa, K. (2004). *Barefoot gen.* San Francisco: Last Gasp.

OSPI. (2007). Social Studies Overview. Retrieved October 11, 2007, from http://www.K12.wa.us/CurriculumInstruct/SocStudies/

Publishers Weekly. (2007). The Beat. Retrieved October 11, 2007, from http://pwbeat.publishersweekly.com/blog/2007/02/

Stamaty, M. (2004). *Alia's mission: Saving the books of Iraq.* New York: Knopf.

Index